CW00470918

The A to Z of Innovation Management

The A to Z of Innovation Management

Dr Mike Kennard

The Essential Guide to 26 Key Innovation Management Theories, Models and Frameworks

Published by McKastle

A CIP catalogue record for this book is available from the British Library.

ISBN 978-1-9996823-0-9 (Paperback)
ISBN 978-1-9996823-1-6 (Hardback)

Book layout and design by Clare Brayshaw

Prepared and printed by:

York Publishing Services Ltd
64 Hallfield Road
Layerthorpe
York YO31 7ZQ

Tel: 01904 431213

Website: www.yps-publishing.co.uk

Contents

Introduction

Innovation is the process that generates value through the creation, development, and implementation of new technologies, products and services. For commercial organisations value may be expressed as increased market share, revenues, profit or shareholder returns. For public sector organisations value is focused on improved efficiency and enhanced service delivery.

Processes need to be managed, and therefore innovation is a management task. This comes as something of a surprise to many organisations. Some believe that innovation is a mysterious phenomenon that occurs randomly as a series of 'light bulb' moments. Others believe that innovation can be achieved by throwing copious amounts of money into a room full of boffins, microscopes and whiteboards and then standing well back. Good luck with these approaches. A few organisations believe that innovation is not required at all, and instead focus on relentless cost cutting. They then receive an unpleasant surprise when their customers eventually leave for innovative competitors who can better serve their needs.

In order to better understand and (hopefully) avoid these pitfalls Innovation Management has become a rapidly growing area of interest for both management practitioners and academic researchers. This can be demonstrated by the steady increase in specialist journal and book publications, conferences, and the rise in innovation focused university courses. However, this expansion has made it increasingly difficult to keep abreast of the key developments in the field and the sometimes bewildering array of new terminology.

The purpose of this book is to provide a concise and accessible overview of the key theories, models and frameworks that shape our current understanding of Innovation Management. To make it a bit more engaging (and as a challenge to myself) each key insight corresponds to a letter of the alphabet, giving *The A to Z of Innovation Management*. You can therefore read from start to finish (recommended), or use the book as a reference source, dipping in and out of specific topics as required. What I do hope is that as you get deeper into the book the patterns and linkages between the various concepts will begin to emerge and make sense.

The book is designed to be a key text for Business, Management, Engineering and Technology students studying Innovation Management based courses, particularly at Masters and MBA level. In addition, the book is also suitable for professional managers, executives and directors charged with 'innovating' (this means you). An important feature of the book is that it is solidly grounded in the innovation literature, introducing the reader to the key research underpinning each innovation insight, together with practitioner examples and suggestions for further reading. The final section highlights five broader Innovation Management themes for future development. So enough with the introduction, let's get started...

Ambidexterity

A: AMBIDEXTERITY

A is… not for Apple Inc. This may appear to be sacrilege for a book on innovation, and if you find this too distressing then you can fast-forward to the letter J, where order is restored. Instead we kick the book off with Ambidexterity, defined as the ability of an organisation to be efficient in its management of today's business demands while simultaneously being adaptive to changes and new opportunities in the business environment. This might be easy to say, but is invariably difficult to achieve in practice. Ambidexterity is a concept that goes right to the heart of Innovation Management, and therefore an appropriate place to start our journey.

The term Organisational Ambidexterity was first used in 1976 by Professor Robert Duncan[1] but gained traction following Professor James March's 1991 seminal paper 'Exploration and Exploitation in Organizational Learning'. Since then a body of research suggests that ambidextrous firms are more adept at managing the internal tension and conflicting demands between allocating resources to run the business while dedicating sufficient resources to develop new products and services that can meet future customer requirements. Managing the current needs of the business is said to require an Exploitation mindset. Focusing on developing future opportunities is said to require an Exploration mindset.

Early studies suggested that balancing these trade-offs within the organisation was unachievable, and firms should focus on only performing one of these at a time. However, more recent research proposes that not only can the balance be achieved, but that it is essential for success in the medium term and for survival in the longer term. Examples of the consequences of failing to achieve this balance include Kodak,[2] whose failure to adopt new digital technologies led to loss of market share to competitors like Fujitsu and eventual bankruptcy.

However, Exploitation of the firm's resources to serve the existing market is still an important consideration. It is this which generates revenues and cash flow, allowing the firm to pay staff and creditors. Firms that fail to have a tight focus on cash flow, particularly small to medium enterprises (SMEs), tend to go out of business quickly. Larger publicly listed companies are required to meet short-term quarterly performance targets for their investors, who normally demand steady and consistent growth and are happy to fire chief executives who fail to deliver this. For these reasons most companies have a strong focus on Exploitation via operational efficiency and execution, demanding a significant degree of resource and executive attention.

Exploration requires a very different approach involving search, experimentation and discovery. Exploration is more speculative and has less predictable outcomes, requiring a higher tolerance for risk and ambiguity. It also does not deliver immediate returns, requiring investment over a sustained period of time before revenues and profits are generated. For these reasons it can be much more difficult to make the case for investment in Exploration in the face of the pressing current needs of the business.

So, the question that researchers have focused on is essentially a very practical one; 'What can firms actually do to achieve ambidexterity and balance the demands of both Exploitation and Exploration?' From this line of enquiry two key areas have emerged: Structural and Contextual Ambidexterity.

1. Structural Ambidexterity

Structural Ambidexterity examines how the internal and external configuration of the organisation can be optimised to develop ambidexterity.[3] Traditional configurations such as the simple functional structure are efficient in allocating resources to support the current business, i.e. Exploitation. However, the inherent rigidity of the functional structure can limit Exploration activities. The formation of cross-functional teams operating within the organisation but outside of the existing management hierarchy can be an effective solution for delivering Exploration within a functional structure.

A second option is to establish formal business units alongside existing functions specifically to manage Exploration, for example research and development (R&D) and business development departments. This has the advantage of having clearly dedicated resource separated from the firm's day-to-day activities. However, there is a danger that these units can become isolated from the wider organisation and therefore opportunities for new products and services developed in Exploration-focused business units are not commercialised.

A third option is to establish project teams that are not only responsible for exploring new opportunities, but are also responsible for bringing these to market. They mirror the structure of the existing business, with their own manufacturing, sales and marketing functions. In this way there is integration between the Exploiting side of the business and the Exploring side of the business, each with equal weighting and supporting a fully ambidextrous organisation.

A fourth option to consider is the role of organisations that are external to the business. For example, the establishment of joint ventures or strategic outsourcing may facilitate the development of ambidexterity. External relationships can provide a channel to escape the constraints of the internal structure, allowing access to new knowledge, talent, thinking and market opportunities.

2. Contextual Ambidexterity

Contextual Ambidexterity considers the role of the individual in the development of an ambidextrous organisation. In this context individuals range from senior executives to front-line workers, linked by a shared set of behaviours and attributes which together help foster ambidexterity. According to Professors Julian Birkinshaw and Cristina Gibson these include:

- Being action-orientated, taking the initiative and being alert to opportunities beyond the boundaries of their own roles.
- Having networkers, brokers and cooperative team players who seek opportunities to combine their efforts with others.
- Being highly motivated with a tolerance for risk and ambiguity and often act without seeking permission or support from superiors. But don't try this in your first week of work...

Although staff operate with a high degree of independence and autonomy the role of the top management team in developing an ambidextrous organisation is still key. Top management sets the strategic direction of the company, defines the organisational structure, and decides what the balance between Exploitation and Exploration should be. They also develop and define key processes and policies such as recruitment, reward and staff development. Senior management must communicate a compelling company vision to stakeholders, and resolve internal conflicts and disputes over resource allocation.

Managers tasked with developing an ambidextrous organisation need to consider both structural and contextual ambidexterity as complementary factors which must be addressed. The right structure with the wrong behaviours is likely to be ineffective. Similarly, even individuals with the right behaviours can be rendered ineffective without the right structure.

What is clear is that while organisational ambidexterity is difficult to achieve it can deliver enhanced long term performance for organisations that can find the right balance between exploitation and exploration.

SUGGESTED READING:

- **Birkinshaw, J. and Gibson, C.** (2004). Building Ambidexterity into an Organization, *MIT Sloan Management Review*, 45(4), pp. 47–55.
- **Duncan, R.** (1976). The Ambidextrous Organization: Designing Dual Structures for Innovation, In Killman, R.H., Pondy, L.R. and Sleven, D. (eds), *The Management of Organization*, New York: North Holland.
- **March, J.G.** (1991). Exploration and Exploitation in Organizational Learning, *Organization Science*, 2, pp. 71–87.
- **O'Reilly III, C.H. and Tushman**, M.L. (2004). The Ambidextrous Organisation, *Harvard Business Review*, 82(4), pp. 74-81.
- **Raisch, S. and Birkinshaw, J.** (2008). Organisational Ambidexterity: Antecedents, Outcomes, and Moderators, *Journal of Management*, 34(3), pp. 375–409.
- **Raisch, S., Birkinshaw, J., Probst, G. and Tushman, M.L.** (2009). Organisational Ambidexterity: Balancing Exploitation and Exploration for Sustained Performance, *Organization Science*, 20(4), pp. 685–695.

NOTES:

1. For the duration of the book I'll assume that academic theorists are all 'professors', or have since been promoted to professor in recognition of their contribution to the field. That should keep everyone happy.

2. The study of specific organisations to advance theory is a central tenet of business research and teaching, particularly through the development of case studies. But there are dangers in oversimplification. Kodak was once used as an exemplar of success through innovation, due to their defeat of Polaroid in the instant camera market.

3. The impact of organisational structure on innovation is further developed in the next section on Boundaries, so read on...

Boundaries

B: BOUNDARIES

As an organisation grows and becomes more complex it can become increasingly difficult to align and integrate separate business functions, which are often locked in battles for limited budgets and focused on resolving functional issues rather than seeing the bigger picture. This can inhibit innovation, leading to reduced growth and providing opportunities for smaller and more agile competitors to capture market share. The management of organisational Boundaries is therefore a key area of Innovation Management. Much research into this area has focused on the creation and cultivation of Boundary Spanning roles, and how these can help overcome structural barriers to innovation. And if you want a successful career, then positioning yourself as a boundary spanner is a good place to start...

Organisational boundaries occur as a result of internal specialisation, which is designed to improve efficiency and effectiveness. The larger the organisation becomes the greater the degree of complexity and internal specialisation, and the greater the number of internal boundaries. In addition, firms which deliver a number of products and services to different markets and geographic territories also tend to create multiple functions to manage this, and so external boundaries with customers and suppliers also become an important consideration.

Typical functions within the organisation include Central Governance headed by the Chief Executive and Board of Directors, R&D, Operations, Marketing, Sales, Procurement, Finance and (lastly) Human Resources. These can be configured into three basic organisational designs; the Functional Structure, the Multidivisional Structure and the Matrix Structure.

1. Functional Structure

This is the simplest form of organisational design. It typically consists of functionally based departments such as R&D,

Operations and Marketing which then report directly into the office of the Chief Executive. The advantages of this structure include:

- A simple chain of command, with the Chief Executive in close contact with each function. This facilitates rapid decision making and reduces (in theory) bureaucracy.

- Clear definitions of roles and responsibilities for each function. For example, if you are the Director of Operations then you know exactly what your responsibilities are.

- Facilitating the development of specialists at senior and mid-management level. For example, if you are the Director of Marketing then you focus exclusively on this role and build up your experience and competence in this area.

However, the Functional Structure also has disadvantages. The most significant of these is potentially limited coordination, cooperation and communication between the functions, which can operate as independent 'silos'. This makes focusing on strategic issues, such as serving the customer better by introducing innovative products and services, more difficult.

2. Multidivisional Structure

The Multidivisional Structure is an attempt to overcome some of the limitations of the Functional Structure, and in particular be more customer focused. As the name suggests, instead of functions reporting into the Chief Executive separate divisions based on specific products, services or geographical areas are created. Each division operates as a self-sufficient business unit with its own specialist functions, such as Operations, Sales and Marketing. The Managing Director of each division has direct profit and loss responsibility, and is accountable to the Chief Executive for delivering agreed targets (usually in return for a sizable bonus). The advantages of the Multidivisional Structure include:

- A simple chain of command, with the Chief Executive in close contact with each division. This facilitates rapid decision making and reduces (in theory) bureaucracy.

- Being customer focused and performance driven, while also allowing senior and mid-level managers to build up expertise and experience in their specific divisional products, services, and markets.

- Being relatively straightforward to adapt the structure to take advantage of a new business opportunity by simply creating a new division.

- Similarly, being relatively straightforward to close down an underperforming division without having to reorganise the rest of the business.

However, the Multidivisional Structure also has disadvantages. This includes the duplication of functions across each division. For example, if an organisation has six divisions, then there needs to be six Operations Departments, six Finance Departments, six Human Resources departments and so on, leading to inefficiency.

In addition, the performance-driven nature of the Multidivisional Structure can lead to non-cooperation between the divisions, making it difficult to reallocate resources to take advantage of new opportunities. In extreme cases there is a danger of a loss of central control if a large and successful division becomes too dominant.

3. Matrix Structure

The Matrix Structure is an attempt to capture the advantages of Functional and Multidivisional Structures without the associated disadvantages. It works by having multiple customer-focussed projects which draw on specialist resource from centrally managed functions as required. Matrix structures are particularly common in large organisations which are heavily technology dependant and have a wide portfolio of products, services and markets. Advantages of the Matrix Structure include:

- Effective knowledge management, allowing knowledge to be integrated across organisational boundaries.
- The development of functional efficiencies and specialisation while remaining customer focused.
- Being relatively flexible and easy to adapt to changes in the business environment, new technologies and new market opportunities.

However, there are disadvantages. Matrix Structures are highly complex, with role, task, cost and profit responsibilities often unclear. This can lead to confusion, conflict, and endless meetings designed to clarify and agree priorities. This in turn can slow down decision making and reduce organisational agility and effectiveness.

So, it can be seen that whichever organisational structure is selected there are specific internal boundaries which can act as barriers to the transfer of information to various degrees. Boundary Spanning roles therefore have an important part to play in transferring information and knowledge and facilitating innovation. In particular, individuals who can span boundaries between technically focused functions (such as R&D labs and manufacturing units) and commercially focused functions (for example Sales and Marketing) are highly valuable.

Sometimes these boundary spanning roles are formalised into full-time positions, but more often they are informal roles where the individual has made the effort to cultivate a network of contacts between different departments. The effectiveness of an informal boundary spanner will depend on the degree of credibility and influence that they have built up within the organisation. Often this will be rooted in their understanding of technology and how it can be applied to new products and services, combined with good communication skills.

Organisations wishing to develop boundary spanning capabilities can implement a system of regular role rotation between functions and divisions. This allows individuals the opportunity to build up their experience of how different areas perform, and cultivate a network of contacts. Formal management development interventions such as training, professional development and sponsoring executive MBAs can also improve an individual's understanding of how various business functions integrate, as well as providing another opportunity for networking.

While developing boundary spanning individuals is broadly positive, organisations need to be aware that over time boundary spanners will become highly influential, and potentially the gatekeepers of information. Sometimes this can lead to the self-interested filtering and distortion of information, and resistance to new ideas and opportunities that may weaken their powerbase.

B: BOUNDARIES

Can an organisation operate without internal boundaries, and would this stimulate innovation? In 1958 Wilbert 'Bill' Gore turned his back on a 17 year career as an R&D manager at the chemical giant DuPont, and founded W L Gore and Associates (henceforth 'Gore'). What followed over the next 40 years is pretty close to the archetypal American dream, where a business which started out in the family basement became a billion dollar turnover company employing over 7,500 'associates' in over 25 countries. Gore has a worldwide reputation for bringing innovative products to markets as diverse as medical supplies, breathable fabrics (Gore-Tex), guitar strings, dental floss and electronic insulation.

But behind these products is the unique way in which Gore manages innovation. Bill Gore clearly formed a strong opinion on what he felt worked (and didn't work) in terms of organisational design based on his experience at DuPont. When he founded his own company he effectively threw away the rulebook on how companies should be run, and set up a unique and innovative business.

To start with, there are no employees, only associates. There are no job titles, no hierarchy and no managers. New associates are assigned a sponsor, encouraged to find a project that they are interested in, and start work. Leaders are simply people who can convince other people to follow them on a new project. Annual pay rises are set not by management, but by their peers and based on their individual and team contribution.

Recruitment is a lengthy affair, and interviews and appointments are ultimately made by fellow associates. If a division rises above 200 associates then it is split up in order to retain a small company feel. Within each division there are no formal boundaries. The company has core values of fairness, freedom, consultation and keeping commitments. In some ways the company feels like a giant social experiment – but does it work?

B: BOUNDARIES

Well, Gore clearly have developed highly innovative products, and have grown from nothing to a billion dollar turnover company. In addition, the company is routinely voted as one of the best places to work in the countries in which it operates. Can this boundaryless system be copied by other companies? Not unless they are in the start-up phase, according to Bill Gore. Any larger established company would not be able to impose the corporate culture required.

But is this too good to be true? It is difficult to find much negativity or criticism in the literature. But by utilising this unique organisation Gore may be limiting the pool of potential employees. Some people are uncomfortable with ambiguity, they like knowing who their boss is and what their job title is, and don't want their pay set by their colleagues. In short, they feel more comfortable when clear boundaries have been established, leaving them free to focus on their specific role.

The positive role of boundaries in stimulating innovation has been explored by professors Michael Gibbert and Liisa Välikangas in a special issue of the strategy journal *Long Range Planning.* They argue that boundaries focus attention and can motivate and stimulate the discovery of solutions. Boundaryless structures may lack such stimulation, making innovation more difficult. Gibbert and Välikangas expand the definition of boundaries to include resource boundaries such as constraints on time or knowledge, and mental boundaries such as the establishment of project goals, objectives or milestones.

So, it can be seen that achieving an optimal balance between freedom and control (via the establishment of boundaries) is a key area of Innovation Management. This is likely to be contingent on factors such as industry sector, the size and complexity of the firm, and the leadership philosophy. Where there are established organisational boundaries in place the development of formal or informal boundary spanners is an important consideration to facilitate innovation.

B: BOUNDARIES

SUGGESTED READING:

- **Aldrich, H. and Herker, D.** (1977). Boundary Spanning Roles and Organisational Structure, *Academy of Management Review*, 2(2), pp. 217–230.

- **Gibbert, M. and Välikangas, L.** (2004). Boundaries and Innovation: Special Issue Introduction, *Long Range Planning*, 37(6), pp. 495–504.

- **Santos, F. and Eisenhardt, K.** (2005). Organizational Boundaries and Theories of Organization. *Organization Science*, 16(5): 491–508.

- **Tushman, M. and Scanlan, T.** (1981). Characteristics and External Orientations of Boundary Spanning Individuals, *Academy of Management Journal*, 24(1), pp. 83–98.

- **Tushman, M.** (1977). Special Boundary Roles in the Innovation Process, *Administrative Science Quarterly*, 22(4), pp. 587–605.

Clusters

C: CLUSTERS

Why is Silicon Valley so successful, and can this success be replicated in different regions, countries, and industries? Located in the Santa Clara area of Northern California, Silicon Valley has become the home of some of the world's largest high technology companies, including Apple, Cisco, Facebook, Google, Hewlett-Packard, Intel, Oracle, Sandisk and Symantec, along with countless mid-sized companies and entrepreneurial start-ups. In 1997 *The Economist* estimated the GDP of Silicon Valley to be $65 billion[1] – and this was before the explosion of broadband internet, tablets, social media and smartphones. Governments and policy makers around the world have therefore attempted to uncover the secret to creating their very own Silicon Valleys, leading to the development of the economic concept of Clusters.

On first inspection it seems that the companies in Silicon Valley have become successful due to their ability to innovate by bringing new technologies and business models rapidly to market. But does the high density of firms within the same sector and the geographic location itself play an active role in facilitating innovation? Well, the area is home to several excellent universities[2] – for example Carnegie Mellon University, California State University, San Jose State University, Santa Clara University, Stanford University and the University of California – all delivering a steady stream of research outputs and eager science, technology, engineering and business graduates into the local economy.

The area also attracts venture capitalists keen to invest in start-ups that may become the next Apple, the next Amazon, the next Google, the next Facebook, the next... you get the picture. A strong service industry has also developed to support business, for example law firms specialising in areas such as intellectual property, initial public offerings (IPOs) and personal wealth managers (California has the highest concentration of millionaires in the United States). So clearly a combination of factors have interacted and contributed to Silicon Valley's success – but can the precise nature of these interactions be sufficiently well understood and quantified to enable similar clusters to be developed elsewhere?

C: CLUSTERS

According to the late Professor Bennett Harrison, research into Clusters (or 'Industrial Districts') has actually been performed since the 1920s, primarily by economic geographers (yes, there is such a thing). However, it was the publication of Harvard Professor Michael Porter's 1990 book *The Competitive Advantage of Nations* that sparked a rapid increase in research into the field. Porter, as you may know if you have been forced to sit through endless Strategic Management lectures, is best known for his work on firm competitiveness, and in particular his *Five Forces Model*.[3]

As part of his research on firm strategy he developed the concept of *Competitive Advantage*, and so it was perhaps a logical step to see if this could be extended to a national level. In essence, firms compete against each other, and with the advent of globalisation so do nations. Firms and nations that implement policies which generate a competitive advantage over their rivals will be successful; those who don't will end up like Kodak or Greece.

Porter looked closely at why particular industries became successful in certain locations, defining these 'Clusters' as:

> 'Geographic concentrations of interconnected companies and institutions in a particular field.'

Porter proposed a 'Diamond Model' of four broad interrelated elements to help explain the formation of Clusters:

- Factor Conditions: These include human capital, knowledge, plant, finance and infrastructure that are specific to an industry and drive competitiveness.

- Demand Conditions: The size of the domestic market for improved products and services drives innovation and early sales momentum prior to establishing export markets.

- Related and Supporting Industries: These are mutually reinforcing, driving innovation and economies of scope. Examples include computer hardware and software, financial services and legal services, oil refining and plastics manufacturing.

- Firm Strategy, Rivalry and Industry Structure: A high degree of domestic firm rivalry and competition can drive innovation and raise the overall competitiveness of the Cluster.

So, if Porter's diamond was applied to Silicon Valley a positive picture would emerge. Factor conditions are favourable, particularly with the human capital (graduates) and knowledge (research outputs) emanating from the university infrastructure and access to venture capital finance. Demand conditions are also high, due to the large population and wealth of the United States. Related and supporting industries are high, for example hardware, software and legal services. Finally inter-firm rivalry is also high, for example between Apple and Google in the smartphone market, which drives innovation in the functionality and utility of smartphone operating systems.

In addition to these four elements, Porter also acknowledges the role of government. For example, an early boost for high technology firms based in Silicon Valley came from high levels of government defence research spending in the 1960s and 1970s, fuelled by the Cold War and general anti-communist paranoia.

With Porter's diamond framework in place, identifying other successful Clusters becomes straightforward, for example:

- Route 128, Boston, United States (High Technology).

- The Cambridge Cluster or 'Silicon Fen', United Kingdom (Biotech & Computers).

- Bangalore, India (Software Outsourcing).
- City of London, United Kingdom (Financial Services).
- Las Vegas, United States (Gambling, Entertainment, Weddings).
- Digital Media City, South Korea (Media).
- Hollywood, United States (Film & Media).
- Bollywood – Mumbai, India (Film & Media).
- Aerospace Valley, Toulouse, France (Aerospace).
- Napa Valley, California, United States (Wine).
- Tech City, London, United Kingdom (High Technology).
- Milan, Italy (High Fashion).
- Seattle, United States (Grunge Music).[4]
- Paris, France (Overpriced Restaurants).[5]

Can you spot the problem with the above list? Correct. The more you look for Clusters, the more you find them. Porter himself identifies a multitude of Clusters based in the United States, including Clusters for woodworking equipment, jewellery, hosiery, hospital management, golf equipment, office furniture, and (give me strength…) telephone reservation services.

So, it seems irrefutable that Clusters exist and are often economically successful, but is this information useful to anyone, and can a Cluster actually be created as opposed to naturally evolving over time? Certainly governments have attempted to create Clusters, and according to the 2007 Economist article 'The Fading Lustre of Clusters', billions of pounds, euros and dollars have been carefully invested using the following process:

> 'Typically governments pick a promising part of their country, ideally with a big university nearby, and provide a pot full of money that is meant to kick-start entrepreneurship under the guiding hand of benevolent bureaucrats. This has been an abysmal failure – it is companies, not regions that are competitive.'

And yet identifying, supporting and creating Clusters remains a favourite sport of governments and economists alike. Why is this? Perhaps one reason is that governments like to be able to convince the electorate that their policies have had an overall positive influence over the economy, growth and employment. Economists on the other hand like to bring order and predictability to a chaotic world, and are forever trying to forecast how action A will cause outcome B, usually with a degree of accuracy that would make an astrologist blush.[6]

But perhaps this is just human nature. The author Nassim Nicholas Taleb describes what he terms the *Narrative Fallacy*.[7] This is the subconscious tendency of the mind to construct convincing narratives that help us make sense of our environment and to order often random data. Similarly, psychologists have long been aware of 'Illusory Correlation', the phenomena of perceiving a relationship between two or more variables when no such relationship exists.[8] Put simply, when presented with a page full of dots we appear pre-programmed to want to join them up and reveal a pattern, just like when we were children. Cluster theory, it could be argued, falls nicely into this world.

Perhaps this is a fairly sceptical view on Clusters to end on. But it is important to recognise that Clusters do exist and that they can be successful at promoting innovation. My note of caution regards the desirability and effectiveness of state intervention to promote the formation of Clusters – it is up to you to make your own mind up on this point.

SUGGESTED READING:

- **Baptista, R. and Swann, P.** (1998). Do Firms in Clusters Innovate More?, *Research Policy*, 27(5), pp. 525–540.
- **Bell, G.** (2005). Clusters, Networks, and Firm Innovativeness, *Strategic Management Journal*, 26(3), pp. 287–295.
- **Grant, R.** (1991). Porter's Competitive Advantage of Nations: An Assessment, *Strategic Management Journal*, 12(1), pp. 535–548.
- **Hamel, G.** (1999). Bringing Silicon Valley Inside, *Harvard Business Review*, 77(5), pp. 70–84.
- **Martin, R. and Sunley, P.** (2003). Deconstructing Clusters: Chaotic Concept or Policy Panacea?, *Journal of Economic Geography*, 3, pp. 5–35.
- **Porter, M.E.** (1990). *The Competitive Advantage of Nations*, New York: Free Press.
- **Porter, M.E.** (1998). Clusters and the New Economies of Competition, *Harvard Business Review*, 76(6), pp. 77–90.
- **Vaitheeswaren, V. and Carson, I.** (2007). Special Report on Innovation: The Fading Lustre of Clusters, *The Economist*, October 13–19, pp. 20-23.

C: CLUSTERS

NOTES:

1. The *Economist* article 'The Valley of Moneys Delight' was written by John Micklethwait, and published on 27 May 1997. More up to date GDP figures have proved difficult to source, but general data on Silicon Valley and the Californian economy can be found at www.siliconvalleyindex.org and www.ccsce.com.

2. Other universities serving Silicon Valley and the surrounding area include Golden Gate University Silicon Valley Campus, John F. Kennedy University Campbell Campus, Northwestern Polytechnic University (Fremont), Notre Dame de Namur University, San Francisco State University, Silicon Valley University, and University of Phoenix San Jose Campus.

3. Michael Porter's seminal work on strategy is outside the scope of this book, although I promise to include it if I ever write an *A to Z of Strategic Management*.

4. Grunge, lest we forget, was the 1990s music movement pioneered by Seattle bands such as Nirvana, Soundgarden, Alice in Chains, Pearl Jam, and Mudhoney.

5. To be fair, the food is usually quite good…

6. This is a play on the well-known quote from Keynesian economist John Kenneth Galbraith: "The only function of economic forecasting is to make astrology look respectable". So if you are an economist, don't get too cross – some of my best friends are economists.

7. Taleb's book *The Black Swan* explores the errors that are made when attempting to evaluate the probability of certain events occurring (such as financial market shocks). In summary, we don't do a very good job at this due to cognitive limitations.

C: CLUSTERS

8. The term 'Illusory Correlation' was coined by the husband and wife team of Loren and Jean Chapman in 1967. It is one example of a number of cognitive biases which inhibit our ability to make sound judgements and decisions.

Disruptive Innovation

D: DISRUPTIVE INNOVATION

What do the bow and arrow, the sailing ship and the compact disc all have in common? The answer is that they have all been superseded by new disruptive technologies (gunpowder, propeller propulsion systems and internet downloads). Harvard Professor Clayton Christensen's research on Disruptive Innovation is one of the cornerstones of Innovation Management, exploring how organisations can both seize opportunities to disrupt existing markets and avoid falling victim to Disruptive Innovation themselves.

Christensen first considered disruption in his 1995 Harvard Business Review paper 'Disruptive Technologies: Catching the Wave', co-authored with Joseph Bower. His breakthrough came two years later with the publication of the book *The Innovator's Dilemma*. For added appeal it came with a subtitle guaranteed to strike fear into even the most hardened corporate executive; 'When new technologies cause great companies to fail'. And they bought the book in droves, helping notch-up over 200,000 sales to date. To provide some perspective, that's about 195,000 more copies than most business books sell!

This in itself highlights a particular human behavioural trait important to our understanding of Innovation Management. When given a choice, most people would prefer to avoid failure than achieve success.[1] For many, failure is mentally and financially traumatic and should be avoided at all costs. Therefore a book offering guidance on how to avoid failure is likely to be more attractive than one offering guidance on how to achieve success. Although we can't turn back the clock it would be interesting to see how successful Christensen's book would have been if it had been titled *The Innovator's Opportunity – How to succeed with new technology.*[2]

Of course, if Christensen had retitled his book and sold only 5,000 copies then this would have been a great loss, because it has some excellent insights into the practical difficulties of managing innovation in the face of rapidly advancing technology. In the book Christensen focuses on Disruptive Technology, although his later work on business growth replaces this with the term Disruptive Innovation, defined as:

> 'An innovation that helps create a new market and eventually disrupts an existing market, often by displacing an earlier technology.'

Christensen distinguishes Disruptive Innovation from what he terms Sustaining Innovation, defined as:

> 'An innovation that does not create new markets, but enables firms to compete more effectively by offering improvements to existing products or services.'

Sustaining innovations are mainly small incremental improvements to existing products or services. However, they can also be more ambitious in scope, delivering breakthroughs in performance, leapfrogging the competition and allowing the firm to charge higher prices. In contrast, Disruptive Innovations are often simpler, more convenient and lower-priced products or services, which appeal to new or less demanding customers. But once the Disruptive Innovation gains traction in the market it becomes rapidly developed, appealing to more demanding customers and eventually destroying the incumbents.

New technology *per se* is not necessarily disruptive. Christensen gives the example of the first automobiles, which did not disrupt the transportation market because they were so expensive that only the very rich could afford them. However, the Ford Model T was a Disruptive Innovation because it was the first affordable automobile, and therefore disrupted the transportation market. Henry Ford's development of the efficient production line for assembly operations dramatically reduced the cost. Simultaneously Ford paid his workers a high (for the time) $5 per day, ensuring that they could afford to buy the Model T, therefore rapidly developing the adoption of this Disruptive Innovation.[3]

D: DISRUPTIVE INNOVATION

So, now that we understand the distinction between disruptive and sustaining innovation it should be relatively straightforward to manage them effectively. Unfortunately it's not that simple! According to Christensen, the dilemma faced by innovators is that the failure to spot the opportunities and threats posed by Disruptive Innovations can be caused by the organisation's pursuit of good management practices. Yes, you read that correctly – good management practice such as staying close to customers, developing new products and services to precisely to meet their needs (sustaining innovation), and focusing on maximising prices, profits, and share price can all make a company vulnerable to game-changing competitors with Disruptive Innovations.

Let's take just one of these elements – staying close to the customer. This makes a lot of sense, because without customers you have no sales, no profits and no business. However, customers are often not the best people to anticipate or express how new technology can better meet their future needs. For example, I happened to grow up when vinyl records were being replaced by compact discs, which were smaller, more resistant to scratches and jumping, and didn't need to be turned over to play side B. Best of all, you could skip the rubbish songs on an album and go straight to you favourites at the press of a button.

However, if at the time you had asked me what new music technology I wanted, I would have said "A CD which is even more scratch resistant and has the capacity to store more songs." I don't think that in 1990 I would have said "Download exactly the songs I want from the internet (what?) onto my smartphone (double what?) for a fraction of the current price." So, for both CD manufactures and the music industry in general staying close to the customer didn't help them to capitalise on new disruptive technology. Instead companies like Napster, Apple, and Spotify, to name but three, were the ones to profit through disruption of the market.

This is not an isolated case. Witness Kodak's failure to respond to the opportunities presented by digital photography, or IBM's failure to move from mainframes into personal computers, or indeed spot that software would become more valuable than hardware – a fact not lost on a certain Mr Gates. The problem with staying too close to customers is nicely summed up by the following quote attributed to Henry Ford:

"If I'd have asked my customers what they wanted, they would have said a faster horse!"

This doesn't mean that companies shouldn't engage their customers to help develop innovation – they just need to engage the right ones (as we shall see later when we cover Eric von Hippel's work on User-Centred Innovation in section U).

So, given the difficulty associated with Disruptive Innovation what advice can be offered to practicing managers? Christensen makes the following suggestions:

- Determine early on whether a new technology has the potential to be disruptive, or will be sustaining only. This is the first step, and although most organisations have processes to identify and manage sustaining innovation not many focus on identifying and managing Disruptive Innovation.

- Don't measure the potential impact of a Disruptive Innovation with the same metrics used to assess sustaining innovation. For example, sustaining innovations always give an improvement in performance. By contrast, Disruptive Innovations are often initially associated with reduced performance (and lower initial profits), but with the potential to create or access new markets.

- Locate the initial market for the Disruptive Innovation. The classic example is the transistor, a technology which only became dominant once a low cost mass market application was identified – the transistor radio. Once this was established the transistor replaced vacuum tube technology in other electronic applications, rapidly making tubes completely obsolete.

- Separate responsibility for developing disruptive technologies from the mainstream business, and keep it independent. This ensures that the disruptive business has dedicated resources and focus, and is not tied to the same short term profit targets of the mainstream business – which it is unlikely to meet in the early years.

- Consider developing disruptive capabilities through acquisitions. For example, in the 1990s Cisco Systems expanded its capabilities quickly and cost effectively through a series of early stage company acquisitions. It was therefore able to compete effectively with companies that had far more established internal technology development capabilities.

- Develop disruptive business models. For example Ryanair used a low cost business model to disrupt the European airline market. Dell used a mass customisation online business model to disrupt the market for personal computers. Music artists such as Trent Reznor[4] are happy(ish) to give away their music for free over the internet, but make substantial revenues from issuing high price limited edition 12″ vinyl box sets for collectors.

So, 30 years after vinyl records fell victim to the disruption of CDs they are now back as part of a new 21st century Disruptive Innovation! It's a funny old world…

SUGGESTED READING:

- **Bower J.L. and Christensen, C.** (1995). Disruptive Technologies: Catching the Wave, *Harvard Business Review*, 73(1), pp. 43–53.

D: DISRUPTIVE INNOVATION

- **Christensen, C.** (1997). *The Innovator's Dilemma: When New Technologies Cause Great Companies to Fail*, Boston, MA: Harvard Business School Press.

- **Christensen, C. and Overdorf, M.** (2000). Meeting the Challenge of Disruptive Change, *Harvard Business Review*, 78(2), pp. 67–76.

- **Christensen, C. and Raynor, M.** (2003). *The Innovator's Solution: Creating and Sustaining Successful Growth*, Boston, MA: Harvard Business School Press.

- **Christensen, C., Johnson, M. and Rigby, D.** (2002). Foundations for Growth: How to Identify and Build Disruptive New Businesses, *MIT Sloan Management Review*, 43(3), pp. 22–31.

- **Danneels, E.** (2004). Disruptive Technology Reconsidered: A Critique and Research Agenda, *Journal of Product Innovation Management*, 21(4), pp. 246–258.

- **Markides, C** (2006). Disruptive Innovation: In Need of Better Theory, *Journal of Product Innovation Management*, 23(1), pp. 19–25.

- **Schmidt, G. and Druel, C.** (2008). When is Disruptive Innovation Disruptive? *The Journal of Product Innovation Management*, 25(4), pp. 347–369.

NOTES:

1. This is an area of Behavioural Economics called Prospect Theory, which is explored further in the section on Risk and Radical Innovation.

2. Perhaps I could have tested this theory by calling this book *The A to Z of Innovation Management: If you don't read this book your company will fail, even if it's really great now*. Or perhaps not.

3. The concept of adoption is developed further in the next section on Early Adopters.

4. Trent Reznor is the singer, songwriter, musician and producer from the Grammy Award winning American Industrial Metal band Nine Inch Nails. But you knew that.

Early Adopters

E: EARLY ADOPTERS

Early Adopters are consumers who embrace new technologies, products and services, providing vital early momentum and traction in the market place. Without Early Adopters innovations cannot achieve the momentum required to break out of their localised niche into the high revenue generating mass market. Early Adopters are key actors in the theory of diffusion,[1] defined as 'the process in which an innovation spreads out over time amongst the members of a social system'. In the commercial world diffusion is effectively the rate and extent to which new innovations penetrate the market.

Many companies, particularly those with a technology focus, believe that innovative products will sell themselves and that the obvious benefits will be widely recognised by the market. Unfortunately, this is rarely the case and even simple, effective and easy to implement innovations can take considerable time to be widely adopted. In his seminal book *Diffusion of Innovations*, Professor Everett Rogers gives an interesting example of this concerning the control of the disease scurvy in the British Navy.

In the early days of long sea voyages, scurvy killed more sailors than war, accidents, storms, and all other illnesses combined. This changed in 1601 when Captain James Lancaster conducted an experiment to evaluate the effectiveness of lemon juice in preventing scurvy. Lancaster commanded four ships sailing from England to India, and gave three teaspoons of lemon juice per day to the sailors of one ship, and none to the sailors of the other three ships.

By the halfway point of the voyage none of the sailors that had been served lemon juice had succumb to scurvy. On the other three ships, 110 out of 278 sailors had died of scurvy. So Lancaster's experiment was an outstanding success, although I'm not sure that the methodology would have been approved by a Research Ethics Committee.

Also, if he thought it would work why not give lemon juice to three ships and have one ship as the control? Or all four ships, and use historical scurvy data as a proxy control? Moving swiftly on, it could be seen that while the cause of scurvy was not scientifically understood, lemon juice was clearly an effective preventative measure, and so was quickly adopted by the British Navy.

Except that's not what happened. Not until 1747, around 150 years later, did the British Navy trial lemon juice as a cure for scurvy. This is not a misprint – 150 years! Now, during this historical period the British Navy had a lot to think about; the French Navy, the Dutch Navy, the Spanish Navy, pirates, colonial trade routes, oak tree supply, cannon technology, vintage port shortages and the list goes on. However, one would have thought the discovery that the single largest cause of sailor death could be eradicated by lemons would have somehow made it through to the Admiralty as a priority.

The 1747 Navy trial, led by the physician James Lind, reconfirmed the effectiveness of lemon juice and also found that oranges were equally effective – so another step forward. And so with this further solid evidence of the effectiveness of citrus fruit in combating scurvy the British Navy adopted their use immediately for all crew on long sea voyages.

Except that's not what happened. It took another 48 years (48!) for citrus fruit to be adopted, and scurvy in the British Navy was finally wiped out 1795 – just in time for the Napoleonic wars, Nelson, Trafalgar and all that. It's just a bit of a shame that it took the British Board of Trade until 1865, a further 70 years, to adopt a similar policy for the crew of merchant ships.

Why did the adoption of this simple and effective innovation take so long? Perhaps there were other potential cures being trialled. Even James Lind was testing different scurvy cures ranging from sea water, vinegar, nutmeg and cider, as well as citrus fruit. Perhaps the British Navy was very bureaucratic and resistant to change (although innovations in ship design and advanced weaponry were readily adopted). Perhaps

Lancaster and Lind were not sufficiently influential to argue their case effectively. Perhaps oranges and lemons were expensive and difficult to acquire in cold rainy Britain and so discounted as impractical (no such problems for the Spanish Navy...).

What this case does show is that without Early Adopters the diffusion of innovations into the mainstream can be significantly restricted. Rogers identifies five adopter categories, each aligned to a different stage of the diffusion process:

1. Innovators[2]

This class of adopters are the pioneers who are the very first to try a new innovation, making up just 2.5% of the total potential market. They typically have a strong interest in new ideas and technology and are willing to take the risk associated with being first. This risk may be both financial and social; financial due to the investment required and social due to the potential for looking a bit foolish if the innovation turns out to be a dud.

Innovators often have a wide and diverse circle of peer networks, facilitating exposure to new ideas. The key role of the Innovator in the diffusion process is that of allowing a new idea to break into the system, and in this respect they can be said to have an important gatekeeper role. So, if you are launching a new innovation into the market you need to think very carefully about who the 'Innovator' adopters are, and how to reach them.

2. Early Adopters

Early Adopters are the next 13.5% of the market, one step behind the Innovators, but only just. This adopter category has the highest level of opinion leadership, and individuals in this category are considered 'the person to check with' by other potential adopters before they make their own purchasing decisions, hence their importance.

Early Adopters are respected by their peers for their successful use of new innovations, and know that to protect this position they must continue to make wise adoption decisions. In many senses the Early Adopters put their seal of approval on an innovation and help trigger the critical mass that an innovation needs before it can enter the mass market.

In this respect Early Adopters can make or break an innovation, and must be carefully identified and engaged when a new innovation is launched into the market.

3. Early Majority

The Early Majority are more conservative than either the Innovators or Early Adopters, and make up the next 34% of the market. So, when the Early Majority start to buy your new innovation you know that you are at last breaking into the mass market and all your effort in developing and launching your innovation is about to pay off.

The Early Majority may deliberate for some time before adopting a new innovation, and look closely to the Early Adopters for guidance. In this sense they lose the commercial advantage of using a new innovation first, but reduce their risk of adopting an innovation which subsequently fails.

4. Late Majority

The Late Majority have a sceptical and cautious view on new innovations, and only adopt them once they have a proven track record. Often it is the pressure of peers or economic necessity which causes them to adopt, but only after at least half the market has already adopted.

Sometimes the Late Majority have scarce financial resources, and feel that most of the uncertainty and risk associated with an innovation must be removed before they adopt. That said, the Late Majority also make up 34% of the market and so are therefore an important segment to attract.

5. Laggards

A Laggard is the type of student that is always late to my innovation and strategy lectures, despite knowing that my lectures are in fact very interesting and will help them succeed in their career.

But we digress. Rogers defines Laggards as the last 16% in a social system to adopt an innovation. They are highly risk averse, suspicious of innovations and resistant to change. They have long decision making processes, which are often emotionally anchored by past decisions.

Laggards tend to have a limited social network, preferring to hang out with other Laggards and, one imagines, grumble about how quickly the world is changing. If you are launching a new innovation then trying to appeal to Laggards is a waste of resources. Focusing on Early Adopters is the key to success. And if you are a Laggard then keep reading this book, it might just cure you...

SUGGESTED READING:

- **Geroski, P.** (2000). Models of Technology Diffusion, *Research Policy*, 29(4/5), pp. 603–625.
- **Mahajan, V. and Muller, E.** (1998). When is it Worthwhile Targeting the Majority Instead of the Innovators in a New Product Launch? *Journal of Marketing Research*, 35, pp. 488–495.

- **Ram, S. and Jung, H.** (1994). Innovativeness in Product Usage: A Comparison of Early Adopters and Early Majority, *Psychology and Marketing*, 11(1), pp. 57–67.
- **Rogers, E.M.** (1958). Categorizing the Adopters of Agricultural Practices, *Rural Sociology*, 23(1), pp. 345–354.
- **Rogers, E.M.** (2003). *Diffusion of Innovations*, 5th ed., New York: Free Press.

NOTES:

1. Some of you may be thinking that Diffusion itself is a pretty big Innovation topic, and should merit its own special place as 'D' in *The A to Z of Innovation*. Well, there is a good argument for this, but personally I felt that Disruptive Innovation deserved this spot. Anyway, if I didn't fit in Early Adopters then I'd have to use 'Edison' as the 'E' and talk about light bulbs, and nobody wants that.

2. Yes, I agree. This isn't the best terminology ever devised, potentially leading to confusion between 'Innovators' as the developers of innovative products and services and 'Innovators' as the initial adopters of innovative products and services.

First Mover Advantage

F: FIRST MOVER ADVANTAGE

Being the first to bring a new innovative technology, product or service to market can generate significant competitive advantages, for example by allowing the pioneering company to build up sales, market share and brand equity before followers enter the market. Once these advantages have been established the pioneer can enjoy a dominant position as the followers struggle to play catch-up – a First Mover Advantage. However, history shows that utilising a first mover strategy does not guarantee success, and in fact a Fast Follower strategy can often prove more effective. Examples of firms that have won and lost with a first mover strategy are shown below:

First Mover Winners:

◆	Ford:	Affordable Automobile
◆	Intel:	Microprocessor
◆	Pilkington:	Float Glass
◆	Rolls-Royce:	Jet Engine
◆	WL Gore:	Breathable Fabric (Gore-Tex)
◆	3M:	Scotch Tape

First Mover Losers (and Successful Fast Follower):

◆	De Havilland:	Jet Aircraft	(Boeing)[1]
◆	NCSA Mosaic:	Internet Browser	(Microsoft)
◆	IBM:	Smartphone	(Apple)
◆	Raytheon:	Microwave Oven	(Samsung)
◆	Digital Research:	PC Operating System	(Microsoft)
◆	Magnavox:	Gaming Console	(Nintendo)

It can be seen that there are both First Mover Advantages and First Mover Disadvantages, and therefore Market Entry Timing is one of the key strategic decisions that firms must take.

F: FIRST MOVER ADVANTAGE

The academic study of First Mover Advantages can be traced back to the 1950s.[2] However, interest in the area was spurred by Stanford Professors Marvin Lieberman and David Montgomery with the publication of their seminal 1988 paper 'First Mover Advantages' in the prestigious *Strategic Management Journal*.[3] This established many of the frameworks that have been subsequently explored by innovation, strategy and marketing scholars. Lieberman and Montgomery define First Mover Advantage simply as:

> 'The ability of pioneering firms to earn positive economic profits.'

They propose three broad mechanisms that can lead to a First Mover Advantage; technological leadership, pre-emption of scarce assets, and buyer switching costs.

1. Technological Leadership

First movers can gain advantage through technological leadership, which can be achieved by investments in R&D, joint ventures or acquisitions. Technological leadership generates an advantage in two ways; the Learning Curve and Patents.

- Firstly, a cost advantage can be achieved through the Learning Curve, sometimes referred to as the Experience Curve. The Learning Curve model was introduced in the 1970s by the Boston Consulting Group. It predicts that unit production costs fall as cumulative output increases due to experience and learning leading to improvements in efficiency. This in turn generates a sustainable costs advantage for the pioneering firm if learning can be kept proprietary. A cost advantage allows the pioneering firm to offer customers lower prices, therefore maintaining their attractiveness in the market compared to higher priced new entrants.

- Secondly, a pioneering firm with technological leadership can maintain an advantage over new entrants if the technology (or intellectual property) can be protected through Patents. These prevent new entrants from reverse engineering and then copying the pioneer's technology for their own products. The pioneer will therefore retain their advantage until the patent expires, which is usually after 20 years.[4]

2. Pre-Emption of Scarce Assets

First movers can gain advantage through the acquisition of scarce assets before their rivals, thus generating a sustainable advantage. These assets fall into two broad categories; input factors and spatial assets.

- Input Factors can include a wide range of assets, including natural resources (for example rare earth metals), skilled labour, plant, manufacturing equipment and prime retailing locations. By pre-empting rivals in securing these types of input factors an advantage over would-be followers can be achieved, hopefully deterring new entrants.

- Spatial Assets are important in markets where there is only room for a limited number of profitable firms, so the first mover can occupy an attractive position and deter new entrants. Space can be considered in terms of geographic location, the degree of market specialisation, or factors such as limited retailing shelf space for certain product categories. For example, if you want to introduce a new brand of breakfast cereal then you will need to persuade retailers that they should reduce the amount of Kellogg's Cornflakes that they stock – not an easy task.

3. Buyer switching costs

First movers can gain an advantage by establishing high buyer switching costs, making it less likely that the buyer will drop the First Mover for a new entrant. Switching costs can broadly be categorised as Transactional Costs, Learning Costs, Contractual Costs and Psychological Costs.

- Transactional Costs are related to the investment that a buyer must initially make before changing supplier, including negotiations, performing credit checks, product trials and tests, and retraining staff to use the new product.

- Learning Costs are incurred when the buyer adapts to the characteristics of the product over time and therefore is reluctant to change. For example, a lecturer who has built their courses around a specific textbook will be reluctant to use a new textbook (even if it is superior and/or cheaper) because they will have to rewrite and re-plan all of their lectures.[5]

- Contractual Costs are incurred when the supplier has either directly or indirectly built in contractual costs to changing supplier. An example of a direct contractual cost would be an exclusivity clause for an agreed period of time. An example of an indirect contractual cost would be loyalty card schemes such as frequent flyer programmes that make buyers reluctant to switch supplier.

- Psychological Costs are related to the reluctance of buyers to change suppliers due to the risk and uncertainty involved. First movers can build up psychological costs by developing their positive brand attributes such as quality, reliability, value for money and excellent customer service. For many years IBM salesmen would play on this, closing deals by looking the customer in the eye and saying 'Nobody ever got fired for buying IBM!'

Lieberman and Montgomery also considered the factors that can cause First Mover Disadvantages. They propose four primary mechanisms; Free-Rider Effects, Technological and Market Uncertainty, Shifts in Technology or Customer Needs and Incumbent Inertia.

- Free-Rider Effects are said to occur when new entrants benefit from the pioneer's investment in areas such as technology development, infrastructure development, market development and buyer education, thereby reducing their own costs and development time. For example, late entrants to the electric car market will benefit from increased consumer acceptance and the establishment of a network of recharging points.
- Technological and Market Uncertainty are major risks associated with product launches. It is the first movers who must accept these risks prior to launch. Fast followers can gain an edge by a 'wait and see' strategy, and either delay entry until problems are resolved, or decline to enter at all if problems are significant – in both cases saving a considerable amount of their own time and money.
- Shifts in Technology or Customer Needs can make a first mover's offering obsolete, leaving the 'wait and see' followers in the prime position to capitalise on these shifts.
- Incumbent Inertia occurs when the first mover becomes locked into focusing on their existing offering due to organisational inflexibility, reluctance to cannibalise existing product lines, or reluctance to invest in new technologies and plant. These factors inhibit the ability of the firm to respond to new environmental or competitive threats (such as shifts in technology of customer needs).

So, given that there are both First Mover Advantages and Disadvantages, and many examples of winners and losers, how useful is the concept of First Mover Advantage to practicing managers? There are certainly limitations to the concept, and in today's fast moving and globalised economy can there ever be a definitive classification of what a first mover actually is?

For example, if a firm enters an established market but with a new technology, should it be classified as a first mover? What is the minimum size and duration of a first mover's market share before it is considered a 'winner'? And is profit a better measure of success than market share? For example, all of the 'winners' given in the introduction were pioneers in their markets, but today are experiencing significant competition and reduced market share.

Similarly, when considering the list of 'losers' was it the first mover strategy that was flawed, or was it poor execution[6] of the strategy that allowed followers to enter and then overtake the pioneers? And how important is the industry context in determining strategic outcomes – is it appropriate to compare the aerospace sector with microprocessors, software and consumer goods?

In my view, the enduring strength of the First Mover Advantage concept is that it forces firms to actively consider how innovation integrates with the wider business and commercial strategy of the firm. This in turn influences how the firm invests in resources and capabilities.

For example, it is no good adopting a fast follower strategy if the firm lacks the capability to systematically observe and analyse market and technology trends and respond rapidly to successful pioneers with competing products. Similarly, pursuing a first mover strategy in technology driven markets is unlikely to be successful without a significant investment in R&D, a commercial function that can rapidly grow market share (before fast followers can respond) and an organisational culture with a relatively high tolerance of risk (because not all first mover products or services will succeed).

Larger organisations with a wide portfolio of products, technologies and markets may choose to utilise both first mover and fast follower strategies simultaneously. Smaller organisations may decide that they can't afford to conduct the large amounts of R&D and market research required to be pioneers, and therefore adopt a fast follower strategy where their costs of entry into an already established market are reduced.

So, while the first mover advantage concept has its limitations I'd argue that it is still a valuable addition to the Innovation Management toolkit.

SUGGESTED READING:

- **Boulding, W. and Christen, M.** (2008). Disentangling Pioneering Cost Advantages and Disadvantages, *Marketing Science*, 27(4), pp. 699–716.
- **Kerin R., Varadarajan, R. and Peterson, R.** (1992). First Mover Advantage: A Synthesis, Conceptual Framework, and Research Propositions, *Journal of Marketing*, 56(4), pp. 33–52.
- **Lieberman, M. and Montgomery, D.** (1988). First Mover Advantages, *Strategic Management Journal*, 9, pp. 41–58.
- **Lieberman, M. and Montgomery, D.** (1998). First Mover (Dis) Advantages: Retrospective and Link with the Resource Based View, *Strategic Management Journal*, 19(12), pp. 1111–1125.
- **Shankar, V., Carpenter, G.S. and Krishnamurthi, L.** (1988). Late Mover Advantage: How Innovative Late Entrants Outsell Pioneers, *Journal of Marketing Research*, 35, pp. 54–70.
- **Suarez, F. and Lanzolla, G.** (2005). The Half Truth of First Mover Advantage, *Harvard Business Review*, 83(4), pp. 121–127.

F: FIRST MOVER ADVANTAGE

NOTES:

1. The De Havilland Comet was the first successful commercial jet aircraft, before a series of tragic accidents caused by metal fatigue led to the grounding of the fleet and the rise of Boeing with their 707 model. However, even without the accidents it is unlikely that the Comet would have survived in the face of the Boeing challenge due to simple economics – the B707 carried between 140 and 190 passengers compared to between 40 and 80 passengers for the Comet, giving Boeing a decisive commercial advantage.

2. First mover advantages are discussed in Main, O. W. (1955) *The Canadian Nickel Industry*, Toronto: University of Toronto Press. Let me know if you have read any earlier work for inclusion in the 2nd edition.

3. Lieberman and Montgomery's classic paper went on to be awarded the 1996 prize from the Strategic Management Society, and prompted them to publish a retrospective paper on First Mover Advantage in 1998.

4. The effectiveness of Patents in protecting innovation and preventing imitation is discussed in section P.

5. This is why *The A to Z of Innovation Management* is positioned as a book to complement and support existing courses and their textbooks, not to replace them.

6. Execution of strategy is of course a vital, yet sometimes overlooked, determinant of success. As the saying goes, 'An average strategy with excellent execution will beat an excellent strategy with average execution.' Luck, serendipity and perseverance also influence business outcomes more that many would like to admit.

Gazelles

G: GAZELLES

A gazelle is a member of the antelope family typically found in the harsh environment of the African savannah. Living on a diet of plants and leaves, gazelles are well known for their agility and speed, with the ability to run in bursts of up to 60 miles per hour. This enables them to evade the many predators that also inhabit the savannah and have a taste for gazelle steak. So far so good. A Gazelle is also the name given to small high growth companies that account for the majority of new job creation, and the concept forms a major linkage between the fields of innovation, economics and entrepreneurship.[1]

The term 'Gazelles' was coined by the American academic David Birch. Birch was a physics student at Harvard in the 1960's who was forced to sit through an Introduction to Economics module, perhaps as a punishment. Here he was taught about the economist's rational world of perfect information where firms acted in an identical way to minimise costs and maximise benefits. However, as the son of a businessman, Birch felt that the perfect world of the economist did not square with his own experiences, and set about using his physics training to study firms at the individual level (the atoms) and find out what was really going on.

How many firms do you think Birch studied? A thousand? A hundred thousand? A million? Well, in the 18 year period between 1969 and 1987 Birch and his team studied 12 million businesses, accounting for between 90% and 95% of all private sector employment in the US. The good news is that this Herculean effort yielded some startling results that even now form the bedrock of our understanding of entrepreneurship and significantly influence government policy on employment (employment generally being considered a good thing due to its positive effects on tax receipts, social stability and getting re-elected).

Birch found that instead of firms behaving as a stable homogeneous group there is actually tremendous turbulence, chaos and variation beneath the aggregated data showing overall economic growth or decline. For example, Birch found that every year around 10% of businesses and jobs are lost. Or put another way, every five years, half (yes, half) of all businesses and jobs in the US are lost and must therefore be replaced by new businesses. But which types of business actually generate these jobs? To facilitate the analysis Birch segmented businesses into three distinct groups that he termed Mice, Elephants, and Gazelles.[2]

> Mice: These are the very small businesses where the owners draw an income but are not looking to grow. Examples include shop keepers, garages, electricians, plumbers and self-employed freelancers.
>
> Elephants: These are large companies and corporations with over 500 employees. Elephants have established products, services and customers and are looking to grow, but they typically find that growth is difficult.
>
> Gazelles: These are new businesses that are small but are growing at a high rate due to their development of innovative products, services and business models. It is these Gazelles which are the driver for new job creation.

Birch found that Elephants are often locked into cost cutting and employment reduction through downsizing, rightsizing, outsourcing or offshoring. For example, between 1980 and 1987, Fortune 500 companies laid off 3.1 million people. However, Gazelles are focused on rapid growth by applying technology to create services that often have no hardware product, such as software, finance, education, telecommunications, consulting, healthcare, insurance, and asset management. Growth is fuelled by access to capital, skills, and export markets for these services. The net effect is that during the same 1980 to 1987 period the US actually added 14 million new jobs to the economy despite the Fortune 500 cull.

Birch also proposed that there is an inherent entrepreneurial spirit in the United States that fuels the formation of gazelles. He cites a survey showing that 38% of men and 47% of women would want to run their own business if they could have their dream job, ahead of 'athlete' and 'test pilot' for the men, 'novelist' and 'photographer' for the women (and presumably 'academic' for both men and women).

Birch contrasts this with the situation he perceives in Europe. For example, in Holland, less than 2% of university graduates ever work for a small or medium-sized business. In France, 500,000 jobs from large corporations were lost between 1975 and 1983, but only 50,000 new jobs were created from new businesses in the same period. The recent economic crisis has left Europe with double digit levels of unemployment, particularly youth unemployment, in countries like Spain, Greece and Italy. So, what factors can facilitate new venture creation and growth?

Birch suggests that what is required is a fundamental shift from the notion of job security with a single employer (the soon-to-be extinct 'job for life') to employment security based on the skills and mobility of the individual. Put simply, businesses and nations cannot compete effectively in a dynamic globalised market if they only have a static labour force. They must therefore foster highly skilled, highly flexible and innovative workers who do not have to rely on benevolent corporations or the state for employment.

Where does all of this leave the large corporations (the Elephants), and why can't they do a better job of innovation and growth? After all, they have several major advantages over Gazelles, including higher levels of capital, existing products and services, established customers and brand presence, talented employees (one hopes), plant and infrastructure and significant experience of the market dynamics.

In addition, large corporations tend to have a portfolio of products and services, so if a new product launch fails it is not usually terminal for the business. In contrast, most new businesses focus on developing a single product or service on which success or failure depends. This means that in theory large corporations should be in a stronger position to take risks with introducing new innovative products and services to market.

Berkeley professors John Freeman and Jerome Engel suggest that several factors combine to reduce levels of innovation in large corporations, providing opportunities for agile and innovative Gazelles to seize opportunities and market share. These include:

- Internal competition for budgets and resources, leading to political infighting between managers and which slows down decision making.

- Incentive and reward structures which focus on the sale of existing products and services, not the development of new products and services.

- High levels of risk avoidance, driven by the fear of being perceived to fail with a new innovative product or service.

- The fear that new innovative products and services would cannibalise the sales of existing product lines.

- The fear that developing new technologies might undermine the power base of managers who have forged their reputation with the development of the current technology.[3]

It can be appreciated that these constraints don't apply to Gazelle businesses, which are typically focused on doing one thing right and whose small size and simple structure facilitates rapid decision making in response to market opportunities and threats. The challenge for Gazelles is to maintain their innovative edge as they grow, and avoid becoming the Elephants of the future. Lions perhaps?

SUGGESTED READING:

- **Acs, Z. and Mueller, P.** (2008). Employment Effects of Business Dynamics: Mice, Gazelles and Elephants, *Small Business Economics,* 30(1), pp. 85–100.

- **Birch, D. L.** (1981). Who Creates Jobs?, *The Public Interest*, 65, pp. 3–14.

- **Birch, D. L.** (1989). Change, Innovation, and Job Generation, Journal of Labor Research, 10(1), pp. 33–38.

- **Freeman, J. and Engel, J.** (2007). Models of Innovation: Start-Ups and Mature Corporations, *California Management Review*, 50(1), pp. 94–119.

NOTES:

1. Some academics argue that innovation and entrepreneurship are very closely related. For example, the late Peter Drucker defined innovation as 'the tool of the entrepreneur'. More from Drucker in the Ideation section.

2. Of course, Birch's famous terminology demonstrates the power of visual metaphors in enhancing the 'stickiness' of ideas. He could have termed Gazelle companies 'Small High Growth Innovation Driven Firms', or SHGIDFs for short, but somehow I don't think that this would have had the same impact.

3. For example, in the 1980s the Dutch company Phillips was slow to spot the potential for compact disc technology. The reason? Many senior managers at Philips had built their reputations on the earlier development and commercialisation of magnetic tapes, and were therefore not keen to embrace a new technology that would make these virtually obsolete.

Horizons

H: HORIZONS

Horizons is a management framework proposed by McKinsey & Company consultants Mehrdad Baghai, Stephen Coley and David White in their 2000 book *The Alchemy of Growth*. As the title suggests, they view sustained business growth as an elusive goal for most firms. This is because the focus on managing the present limits investment in future products, services and markets – a theme also addressed in the Ambidexterity literature. They argue that as a firm's business and revenue streams mature it must have other streams ready to take their place, and that to sustain growth there must be a continuous pipeline of new sources of profit. To help manage the pipeline they segment it into mature, emergent and embryonic phases of the business Life Cycle. They refer to these stages as the three horizons of growth:

Horizon 1:

This encompasses the current products, services and markets that the firm competes in. Even when these markets appear mature, continuing innovation can extend their growth and profitability, particularly when combined with efforts to improve operational efficiency and reduce costs. When considering Horizon 1 managers should ask themselves:

- Are our core businesses generating sufficient profits to allow us to invest in growth?
- Can performance and profits be pushed higher over the next few years?
- Is our cost structure competitive with the rest of the industry?
- Are we protected from new competitors, technologies and regulations which could disrupt the market?

Horizon 2:

This encompasses fast moving entrepreneurial ventures within the business which have the potential to rapidly grow, but not without a significant investment in company resources. Horizon 2 is about building new streams of revenue which over time will replace current businesses. A growth focused company needs to develop several of these emerging businesses concurrently to mitigate the risk of market failure, or in other words putting their eggs into different baskets. When considering Horizon 2 managers need to ask themselves:

- Do we have new businesses capable of creating as much value as the current core businesses?
- Are these new businesses gaining momentum in the marketplace?
- Are we prepared to make substantial investments to accelerate their growth?
- Are these new businesses attracting the entrepreneurial talent in our organisation?

Horizon 3:

This encompasses long-term future opportunities. These are more than just ideas; they must consist of real activities, testing, trials, and small investments. Although the majority of these embryonic businesses will not be successful they need to be promising enough that some of them will go on to succeed in becoming at least as profitable as the current core businesses. When considering Horizon 3 managers need to ask themselves:

- Does our top leadership team devote sufficient time to consider long-term growth opportunities?

- Have we developed a portfolio of options for reinventing existing businesses and creating new ones?
- Are we developing effective ways to turn these ideas into new businesses?
- Have the ideas been made tangible with measurable first steps?

The key to achieving sustainable growth is to manage Horizons 1, 2 and 3 concurrently. The authors advocate that the three Horizons framework is cascaded throughout the organisation, so that every manager focuses on the short, medium and long-term development of their business unit. The authors claim to have demonstrated the effectiveness of the three Horizons framework by studying 30 high growth companies in various industries and geographical territories.

At the time of writing some of these companies are still regarded as successful, for example SAP, Walt Disney, Johnson & Johnson, Bombardier, Charles Schwab and GE Capital. Others however have not fared so well. Nokia has found it difficult to compete against Apple and Samsung, and has now been acquired by Microsoft. Compaq struggled to compete with Dell's innovative business model and has been acquired by HP, itself a company struggling with growth. And as for Enron? Let's not go there!

The lesson perhaps is that there is no 'silver bullet' model or framework that guarantees sustained growth in today's hypercompetitive global markets that are characterised by high levels of change, risk and uncertainty. That said, the Horizons framework is certainly based on common sense and as such is a useful tool for managers.

The central idea of managing a portfolio of innovation projects across different timeframes is an enduring one and has been developed by other authors. Geoff Moore used his experience as an innovation consultant at Cisco to develop some practical insights into how to manage the three Horizons:

- Ensure that the organisation establishes clear boundaries between each Horizon to ensure that the performance of emerging Horizon 2 businesses are not measured against mature Horizon 1 businesses.
- Consider acquisitions in the short term to help fill the Horizon 2 portfolio. This is a quick and often cost effective way of developing new growth opportunities.
- Focus on developing whole new businesses, not just new products, to improve the chances of commercial success.
- Focus on dominating a niche market where the new Horizon 2 business solves a mission critical problem and can quickly build its market share, profits and brand.
- Leadership, not finance, is the most important and scarcest resource for developing Horizon 2 businesses. Ensure that the organisation properly recognises and rewards Horizon 2 leaders to attract experienced and entrepreneurial leaders.

Bansi Nagji and Geoff Tuff, two consultants from Monitor Group, developed a variation on the portfolio approach to Innovation Management with their three level matrix:

Core:	Optimising existing product range for existing customers
Adjacent:	Expanding from existing business into 'new to the company' business
Transformational:	Developing breakthroughs and inventing things for markets that don't yet exist

H: HORIZONS

Nagii and Tuff suggest that optimised resource allocation is contingent on industry sector and firm size. For example a mature diversified industrial goods company may adopt a 70/20/10 split between core, adjacent and transformational businesses. However, for a mid-stage technology firm a more appropriate split may be 50/30/20.

Ultimately the strength of the Horizons concept and the general notion of managing portfolios over different timeframes is that it forces managers to confront a painful truth: that the current core business of the firm has a finite life and will eventually die. Active planning is therefore required to explore, nurture and develop the products and services that will become the future core business of the firm and underpin growth and success.

SUGGESTED READING:

- **Baghai, M., Coley, S. and White, D.** (2000). *The Alchemy of Growth*, London: Texere.
- **Moore, G.** (2007). To Succeed in the Long Term, Focus on the Middle Term, *Harvard Business Review*, 85(7), pp. 84–90.
- **Nagji, B. and Tuff, G.** (2012). Managing Your Innovation Portfolio, *Harvard Business Review*, 90(5), pp. 66–74.

Ideation

I: IDEATION

There is no single accepted definition of innovation. This is not necessarily a bad thing, giving scope for practitioners to shape what innovation means in the context of their own organisational challenges. However, there is a broad consensus that innovation starts with ideas, which are then developed and commercialised. But where do these ideas come from? Well, you could lock yourself in a dark room with a blank sheet of paper and a strong cup of coffee and wait for inspiration to strike – the classic 'light bulb' moment. Good luck with that. Alternatively you could utilise Ideation – the creative process of generating, developing and communicating ideas.

There is a critical difference between waiting for ideas to happen and utilising a process for generating ideas. If you place innovation at the heart of your business strategy for growth then just waiting for ideas to happen is unlikely to deliver the results that the business (and its investors) hope for. Utilising a process for generating ideas is much more likely to deliver a steady stream of new innovations in a much more repeatable and predictable manner, providing a more stable platform for growth.

Over the last 50 years one of the most respected business thinkers has been the late Peter Drucker, the Austrian economist who emigrated to the US and went on to become a leading academic and advisor to the Fortune 500. Drucker viewed innovation as a disciplined and systematic process, firmly believing in the old adage that success is 1% inspiration and 99% perspiration. According to Drucker, ideas (and from them, innovation) come from a conscious and purposeful search for opportunities.

He identified seven distinct sources of opportunity for organisations to explore; Unexpected Occurrences, Incongruities, Process Needs, Industry or Market Changes, Demographic Changes, Changes in Perception, and finally, New Knowledge.

I: IDEATION

1. Unexpected Occurrences

Drucker believed that unexpected occurrences are the easiest source of new opportunities. Consider the story of McDonald's, the global fast food franchise. Back in the 1950s, Ray Kroc, the founder of McDonald's, was a sales representative for a manufacturer of commercial milkshake machines. He noticed that one particular restaurant was ordering more machines than any other. When he investigated he found the reason; this restaurant was wearing through their machines at a faster rate than other outlets – an unexpected failure.

Now Kroc could have ignored this and just carried on selling milkshake machines. But he was curious, and on further investigation discovered that the milkshake machines from this particular restaurant were wearing out because they were simply selling far more milkshakes than the norm – an unexpected success. The restaurant was very popular, and Kroc discovered that they had a process driven system for producing food of a highly consistent quality for a low price. Kroc realised that this successful formula could be replicated, went into business with the restaurant owners, and McDonald's was born.

Fast food may sound a bit low tech for a book on innovation, but consider the story of Viagra, the fastest selling drug in history developed by the pharmaceutical giant Pfizer. Viagra was actually developed as a treatment for angina, a heart condition that constricts the vessels that supply the heart with blood. However, during extensive trials the Pfizer team noticed something unexpected; trial participants seemed rather reluctant to hand back unused pills to the researchers. How strange!

On closer investigation the researchers found that there was an interesting side effect that trial participants had not previously mentioned; enhanced libido and sexual performance. With this new insight Viagra quickly became the leader in the market for erectile dysfunction, generating billions of dollars in revenues for Pfizer.

2. Incongruities

An incongruity is something that seems out of place or strange for a given situation or environment. For example, a student constantly checking Facebook and Instagram on their smartphone during my extremely interesting and thought-provoking innovation lectures is an incongruity. But we digress. Drucker argued that incongruities are rich opportunities for innovation if we can identify them.

For example, in the first half of the 20th century the shipbuilding industry focused on making ships faster or more fuel efficient based on the assumption that these two factors drove the economics of the industry. However, the reality was that the major costs and inefficiencies were actually tied up in the idle time ships were moored in ports waiting for goods to be unloaded and loaded. By identifying the incongruity between the assumptions and the reality of ocean shipping economics shipbuilders focused on designing roll-on roll-off and container ships, dramatically reducing time in port and turning ocean shipping into a major growth industry.

3. Process Needs

A process need is simply a problem that may seem 'obvious' but for which a solution has not yet been designed. If you have ever said "If only someone would invent a ...", then this means that you have identified a process need, and maybe YOU could design a solution (and reap the reward). An example is the development of the reflective 'cat's eye' that helps drivers see the road ahead at night.

Before the development of the cat's eye, roads would either be unlit and extremely dangerous at night, or would need to have mains powered street lighting; extremely expensive to install on all of the road network, especially in rural areas. The cat's eye solved this process need; how to significantly improve road safety at night affordably. The British inventor of the cats-eye, Percy Shaw, patented his design which then went on to be widely adopted around the world. Percy retired a wealthy man.

4. Industry and Market Changes

Industry structures and markets are not set in stone, and they often change very quickly. The catalysts for change can be rapid industry growth or changes in regulatory requirements (particularly relaxations). When industry or market changes occur there are big opportunities for innovators to exploit the change. This opportunity is often strengthened because typically incumbent firms can be slow to anticipate change or react to change when it occurs, focusing instead on defending what they already have.

Examples of industry change include deregulation of financial markets (arguably not such a good thing!), privatisation of nationalised industries such as energy and water, and Open Skies; the name given to the liberalisation of the regulations governing the international commercial aviation industry, aimed at creating a competitive free market.

5. Demographic Changes

You might not have noticed, but we are entering an age of unprecedented demographic change, and this opens up a multitude of opportunities for sharp-eyed innovators and entrepreneurs. Demographic changes affecting industrialised nations include growing populations, ageing populations, increasing affluence, migration, and education and skills shortages.

Often the combination of demographic trends can amplify opportunities. For example, ageing populations combined with increasing affluence has led to the emergence of wealthy retirees who have high levels of disposable income, the so-called 'grey pound/euro/dollar'.

Businesses that can offer new services and products to this demographic are likely to be successful. Similarly, an ageing and growing population provides numerous opportunities in the healthcare sector for entrepreneurs that can spot a gap in the market for new innovative products and services. Like Viagra.

6. Changes in Perception

Is the glass half full or half empty? Perceptions of the same phenomena can be vastly different, and identifying changes in perception can open up opportunities. For example, retired people once perceived that their retirement would be fairly sedate, perhaps involving some gardening and visiting the grandkids once in a while. However, in recent years the perception of retirement has shifted to a much more active lifestyle involving travel and fitness – presenting opportunities for new businesses serving this market.

Another example concerns the perception of food. For sure, many consumers still like to reduce their weekly shopping bill, as evidenced by the rise of discount grocers such as Aldi and Lidl. However, certain shoppers are actually prepared to pay more for food that they perceive has superior nutritional value or ethical credentials (or both). This has driven the rise in demand for organic fruit and vegetables and for ethically sourced Fairtrade goods such as chocolate, both sold at a price premium.

Changes in perception may have a significant effect on Higher Education, especially in light of high tuition fees. If students continue to perceive that their degrees lead to higher earnings that offset the fees in the long run then they will continue to enrol. However, if the perception changes and students believe that the benefits no longer outweigh the costs then this would have a significant impact on university revenues, inevitably leading to the closure of some institutions. However, the shifting dynamics in higher education has also seen the rise of cheaper study options such as Distance Learning and MOOCs (Massive Open Online Courses).

7. New Knowledge

Perhaps the best known innovations have been developed as a result of new knowledge – either technological or social. These innovations are often the result of many years' research and investment, but have the potential to be transformational. Historical examples include the printing press, the steam engine, electricity, the silicon chip and the internet. In particular, three key areas of technology are leading to the development of new innovations:

- Materials
- Biotechnology
- Information Technology

> However, it is important to note that new technology in itself is not innovation; it is the application and commercialisation of new technology that is innovation. For example the recent discovery of the 'super-material' graphene[1] by researchers at the University of Manchester in itself is of limited use. It is the application of graphene's unique mechanical and conductive properties that will deliver new innovative products.

If Drucker emphasises a disciplined and systematic approach to ideation then a useful counterweight is the research focusing on how organisational factors such as culture can facilitate ideation. For example, South African researchers Martins and Terblanche have identified five factors that contribute to an organisational culture that supports creativity and innovation:

- Strategy that creates a shared vision and mission focused on developing new innovative products and services.
- Structures that are flexible and promote freedom, autonomy, cooperation and agile decision making.
- Support Mechanisms such as reward and recognition and efficient resource allocation for innovation.
- Behaviours such as risk taking, support for change, managing conflict and tolerance for mistakes.
- Communication that is transparent and based on openness and trust.

This last point on the importance of communication is demonstrated in the success of Pixar, the highly creative animation studio behind films such as *Toy Story, Finding Nemo, The Incredibles, Cars, Wall-E,* and (my favourite) *Monsters Inc.* According to Ed Catmull, co-founder and president of Pixar, a mistake often made is to exaggerate the importance of an original idea in creating a new product. Instead, it is the *development* of the idea through a great team that leads to breakthroughs. The three key principals that facilitate this development are:

- Freedom to communicate by removing hierarchical barriers and trusting people to work together to solve problems.
- Safe to offer ideas and receive constructive feedback from a fresh pair of eyes.
- Staying close to the academic community to gain access to new insights and talent.

So in summary, the challenge for organisations is to develop a Drucker-like systematic process for generating ideas while simultaneously nurturing a culture to support the development of these ideas into commercially viable products and services.

SUGGESTED READING:

- **Drucker, P.** (1985). The Discipline of Innovation, *Harvard Business Review*, 63(3), pp. 67–72.
- **Bjork, J., Boccardelli, P. and Magnusson, M.** (2010). Ideation Capabilities for Continuous Innovation, *Creativity and Innovation Management*, 19(4), pp. 385–396.
- **Catmull, E.** (2008). How Pixar Fosters Collective Creativity, *Harvard Business Review*, 86(9), pp. 65–72.
- **Martins, E. and Terblanche, F.** (2003). Building Organisational Culture that Stimulates Creativity and Innovation, *European Journal of Innovation Management*, 6(1), pp. 64–74.

- **Woodman, R.W., Sawyer, J.E. and Griffin, R.W.** (1993). Toward a Theory of Organizational Creativity. *Academy of Management Review*, 18 (2), pp. 293–321.

NOTES:

1. Graphene is a sheet of pure carbon one atom thick, a hundred times stronger than steel and an efficient conductor of both heat and electricity. In 2010 two researchers from Manchester University, Andre Geim and Konstantin Novoselov won the Nobel Prize in Physics for their experiments which successfully isolated Graphene, initiating a global race to investigate and develop commercial applications that can exploit its unique properties.

Jobs, Steve

J: JOBS, STEVE

OK, OK, I know you wanted Apple Inc. to be the letter A, but I'm sticking with Ambidexterity! Just to recap, Apple is the Silicon Valley based technology company responsible for launching such commercial disasters as the Apple Lisa PC, the Apple Newton Message Pad, the Apple Pippin Games Console, the Apple eMate 300 and the self-destructing Power Mac G4 Cube. In amongst the wreckage Apple also managed to launch some fairly successful products such as the MacBook, iMac, iPod, iPhone, iPad and iTunes, becoming the world's most valuable company in the process. The man credited with Apple's success is co-founder and CEO Steve Jobs,[1] and therefore Jobs is a fitting subject to fill the J slot in *The A to Z of Innovation Management*.

The commercial success of Apple, its steady stream of market defining products, and the untimely death of Jobs in October 2011 from pancreatic cancer, has led to a slew of books and articles analysing his impact on the business. In particular, there has been a focus on identifying and distilling the lessons that can be learned from Jobs on leadership and innovation, with at least 30 books[2] published between 2010 and 2014.

The message seems to be clear; if you want your company to be as innovative and successful as Apple then you must lead like Jobs. Focusing on *Steve Jobs: The Exclusive Biography* by Walter Isaacson (handily summarised in a *Harvard Business Review* paper by the same author) no less than 14 separate 'keys to success' are identified. Although many of these are strongly driven by Jobs's own personality traits, there are five useful insights into innovation at Apple:

1. Focus

It's easy to get distracted with fast-moving technology markets and a company to save from bankruptcy. When Jobs was asked to return to lead Apple in 1997 he found a vast portfolio of different computers and peripherals, including multiple versions of the Macintosh. New product development was eating through cash reserves and customers were confused as to what to buy, so ended up not buying. You don't need an MBA to know that there is only so long that any company can tolerate rising costs and falling revenues.

Jobs saw the danger and took a ruthless approach. Apple was now to focus on developing just 4 'great' products serving well defined market segments. All other products and development programmes were cancelled with immediate effect. The new strategy of choosing what *not* to do worked, and set the platform for future success.

2. Simplicity

Surely innovative technology based products should be complex, expensive and difficult to use without reading some sort of manual. For Apple the opposite philosophy was applied – innovation meant simplifying both hardware and software to make the user experience as easy and intuitive as possible.

Jobs hired Jonathan Ive to head the industrial design team with a clear mandate to simplify Apple products, even extending to product packaging and the design of unseen circuit boards. The result was a new generation of sleek, distinctive and desirable products that came to define the Apple brand (and sell by the truckload at a premium price).

3. Intuition

Jobs believed strongly in his own innate ability to identify breakthrough products and new markets, and bypassed the whole expensive business of conducting market research – in effect becoming a one man focus group relying on intuition rather than mountains of marketing data.

According to Henry Ford (another American industrial icon with a half-decent track record):

"If I had asked my customers what they wanted,
they would have said a faster horse!"

We came across Ford's quote earlier in the book in the section on Disruptive Innovation, and Jobs took this approach to heart, believing that customers don't necessarily know what they want until they are actually shown breakthrough products.

According to Isaacson, Jobs designed products that he wanted to use himself. For example, as a music fan he wanted a simple portable device that could carry a thousand songs – an idea that became the hugely successful iPod.

4. Reinvention

One of the great innovation myths is the belief that you need to come up with brand new, never before seen, and unique products that are inspired through a flash of creative genius. However, it can be equally powerful (and easier, cheaper and lower risk) to follow a path of reinvention and repositioning of existing products.

Apple were not the first company to launch personal computers, MP3 type music players, smartphones or tablets. However, when they did enter these markets they offered products that leapfrogged the competition and positioned themselves as the leaders.

For example, the iPhone was positioned as a premium priced device that was 'way smarter and way easier to use' than any existing smartphone. When launching the iPhone at Macworld 2007 Jobs declared (with a totally straight face) "Today, Apple reinvents the phone!"[3]

5. High Performance Environment

Steve Jobs was a perfectionist, arguably to an obsessive degree. Often an abrasive character, words like 'impatient', 'petulant', 'rough', 'stormy', 'rude', 'terrorising', and 'abusive' have been used to describe his management style – and that was from Isaacson's *Exclusive Biography*, published with the full approval of Jobs! Personally, I don't advocate this style of leadership, although the strong counter argument is that in the case of Apple – 'It got results'.

Getting angry on a regular basis is not in itself a pathway to high performance, although it may make you feel better if you're having a particularly bad day. So Jobs also ensured that he was surrounded by an exceptionally talented, hardworking, and presumably very well remunerated team with a passion to succeed.

As discussed in the section on Clusters, one of the driving factors behind the success of Silicon Valley is that the high density of technology firms generates a highly dynamic market for talent. Employees not happy with Jobs's management style could easily move on to another company, and yet according to Isaacson Jobs had the ability to inspire a high degree of loyalty within Apple.

As well as a focus on talent and individual performance, Jobs was also a strong believer in facilitating informal meetings to promote idea sharing and creativity (as opposed to email, memos and formal PowerPoint presentations). For example, as CEO at Pixar he redesigned the building to encourage unplanned collaborations. The main doors, stairs, and corridors all led to the central atrium where the café and mailboxes were also located. This encouraged mingling and spontaneous meetings between people that otherwise might not come into contact.

J: JOBS, STEVE

Are there wider, more generally applicable skills, traits and behaviours that mark out 'Innovators' such as Steve Jobs, Amazon CEO Jeff Bezos and Dell CEO Michael Dell from mere mortals? This is a question that Professors Jeffrey Dyer, Hal Gregersen and Clay Christensen[4] set out to answer, publishing a summary of their results in the 2009 *Harvard Business Review* paper 'The Innovators DNA'. Perhaps unsurprisingly their answer is 'Yes' – it would have been a pretty dull piece of work otherwise.

Their research was based on extensive data collection and analysis; a six year study of 25 innovative entrepreneurs, and a survey of more than 3,000 executives and 500 individuals who had started innovative companies or invented new products. Phew. They conclude that there are five generic 'Discovery Skills' that innovative leaders leverage to create new ideas:

Discovery Skill 1: Associating

Associating is the ability to successfully connect seemingly unrelated questions, problems or ideas from different fields. Our experience, knowledge and exposure to fresh inputs can trigger new associations, which in turn may lead to novel ideas. This links well into another of Isaacson's observations on Jobs, who looked for ideas at the interfaces between the sciences, humanities and arts (with a bit of Zen Buddhism thrown in for good measure).

Discovery Skill 2: Questioning

Innovative leaders constantly ask the questions "Why", "Why not?" and "What if?" to challenge assumptions and perceived wisdom. For example, Michael Dell asked why a computer cost five times as much as the sum of its individual components. From this he devised an innovative business model that significantly reduced the cost of computers and launched his successful business.

Discovery Skill 3: Observing

Innovative leaders carefully, intentionally and consistently look for small behavioural details in areas such as the activities of customers, suppliers and competitors. These observations generate insights about new ways of doing things.

Discovery Skill 4: Experimenting

Innovative leaders are constantly testing new ideas with small-scale experiments to find out what works and what doesn't before scale up and product launch. They encourage their staff to experiment and share the learning within the organisation, with an open culture that is tolerant of failure.

Discovery Skill 5: Networking

Innovative leaders go out of their way to meet people with different ideas and perspectives to their own knowledge domains. This includes visiting other countries and cultures, attending idea conferences, and mixing with entrepreneurs, academics, politicians and thinkers.

Are there limitations in what we can learn from studying successful innovators? In a word 'yes', even if you read all 30 books on Steve Jobs (not recommended), or conduct an extensive six year research programme. The problem is that when we seek to understand what leads to high performance by studying high performing individuals or organisations our data collection, analysis and interpretations can become distorted by the high performance itself. You may want to read that sentence again. This distortion is called the 'Halo Effect', a phenomena explored in Phil Rosenzweig's book of the same name (and in my opinion essential reading for all managers and business school students).[5]

For example, when we look at a commercially successful leader like Steve Jobs we tend to interpret behaviours, traits and decisions as positive, because we know that ultimately Apple was successful. But imagine for a moment that Apple was commercially unsuccessful. Then we would see Jobs in a quite different light. We would say that his quest for perfection led to costly overruns, his abrasive manner alienated staff and discouraged top talent from joining Apple. His focus on only a handful of products was high risk and led to missed opportunities. And as for ignoring market research and relying wholly on the intuition of one man, well that was just asking for trouble! But because Apple was successful we see these same factors in a positive light.

So, if you want your organisation to be innovative and successful you can gain useful *insights* from how others have led, but you must not blindly follow, or you are likely to experience painful disappointment in the results. The challenge of management is to develop your knowledge, experience and capabilities, and to have the courage to find your own path.

SUGGESTED READING:

- **Dyer, H. Gregersen, H. and Christensen, C.** (2009). The Innovator's DNA, *Harvard Business Review*, 90(4), pp. 92–102.

- **Isaacson, W.** (2011). *Steve Jobs: The Exclusive Biography*, New York: Simon & Schuster.

- **Isaacson, W.** (2012). The Real Leadership Lessons of Steve Jobs, *Harvard Business Review*, April, pp. 93–102.

- **Rosenzweig, P.** (2007). *The Halo Effect and Eight Other Business Delusions that Deceive Managers*, New York: Free Press.

NOTES:

1. In brief, Steve Jobs cofounded Apple in 1976 with Steve Wozniak and Ronald Wayne; was ousted by the board in 1985; founded NeXT and Pixar; and returned in 1997 to lead Apple through its most successful period until his death in 2011 at the age of 56. At the time of his death Apple had become the world's largest company with a market capitalisation of approximately US$337 billion.

2. A small selection of Steve Jobs books – for the full list go to Amazon.com and type in 'Steve Jobs'!

    - *How to Think Like Steve Jobs*, by Daniel Smith.
    - *Steve Jobs: Ten Lessons in Leadership*, by Michael Essany.
    - *The Innovation Secrets of Steve Jobs: Insanely Different Principles for Breakthrough Success*, by Carmine Gallo.
    - *Steve Jobs: Life Changing Lessons! Steve Jobs on How to Achieve Massive Success, Develop Powerful Leadership Skills*, by William Wyatt.
    - *Steve Jobs: Life, Career, Personality, And What Can We Learn From Steve Jobs?*, by Alexander Cooper.
    - *The Steve Jobs Way: iLeadership for a New Generation*, by Jay Elliot.
    - *What Would Steve Jobs Do? How the Steve Jobs Way Can Inspire Anyone to Think Differently and Win*, by Peter Sander.

- *Leading Apple with Steve Jobs: Management Lessons from a Controversial Genius*, by Jay Elliot.

- *Inside Steve's Brain: Business Lessons from Steve Jobs, the Man Who Saved Apple*, by Leander Kahney.

- *You can be as successful as Steve Jobs if you buy my book*, OK, I made this one up, but you get the picture...

3. You can view Jobs's introduction of the iPhone at Macworld 2007 going to Youtube.com and type in 'Steve Jobs iPhone Macworld 2007'. A real masterclass in presentation skills and well worth viewing.

4. Yes, this is the same Clay Christensen whose work we discussed in the section on Disruptive Innovation – well done for noticing!

5. Just to reinforce the point, I can't recommend Rosenzweig's *The Halo Effect* highly enough – but make sure you finish reading *The A to Z of Innovation Management* before you get it.

Knowledge Management

K: KNOWLEDGE MANAGEMENT

Knowledge can be defined as 'the combination of information, experience and skills that leads to the understanding a particular subject'. Knowledge is acquired through both practice and education, and allows us to solve complex problems through creative thinking. The Austrian economist and management guru Peter Drucker[1] foresaw the development of what he termed the *Knowledge Economy*. In the Knowledge Economy growth is dependent on the quantity, quality and accessibility of the information available to 'Knowledge Workers',[2] rather than the means of production such as factories.

This shift in thinking initiated the trend for the outsourcing of production from Western economies to low-cost emerging economies such as China. Western governments have responded by increasing the supply of Knowledge Workers, for example by raising the number of graduates. For firms, the area of Knowledge Management has become increasingly important, particularly in respect to how knowledge drives innovation and competitive advantage.

As observed by South African scholar Marina du Plessis, there are many definitions of Knowledge Management, so in this spirit I offer the following:

> 'Knowledge Management is the organisational system that acquires, stores and provides access to information, experience and expertise in order to create new capabilities, support innovation, and drive performance.'

So, while Knowledge Management (KM) is distinct from innovation it has a major role in developing the capability to innovate. This is achieved in several distinct ways:

- KM provides a focus in the organisation for the value of knowledge, creating an environment for the creation, sharing and leverage of knowledge.

- KM provides the mechanisms for knowledge to be stored and easily retrieved, growing the organisation's overall knowledge base.

- KM can be used to convert Tacit Knowledge (i.e. the knowledge acquired by individuals over time) into Explicit Knowledge (i.e. knowledge that can be written down, retrieved and utilised by any individual).

- KM facilitates collaboration across internal organisational boundaries, for example via online forums and cross-functional knowledge focused projects.

- KM encourages collaboration with external partners who can provide or contribute to the development of new knowledge.

- KM contributes to the development of the competencies and skills required for the innovation process by exposing staff to a wider knowledge base.

- KM assists in the identification of gaps in the knowledge base and provides processes to fill those gaps in order to support innovation.

- KM can facilitate the development of a knowledge driven organisational culture within which innovation can be encouraged.

Implementing Knowledge Management is often a difficult and daunting undertaking. Just how do you capture the knowledge of, for example, a hundred-year-old company with 100,000 employees operating in several distinct global markets? One of the big mistakes is to see Knowledge Management as just another IT project. While IT can help facilitate Knowledge Management, this in itself is unlikely to be successful without anchoring Knowledge Management to the overall strategy and developing an organisational culture aligned with Knowledge Management values.

K: KNOWLEDGE MANAGEMENT

Morten Hansen, Nitin Nohria and Thomas Tierney investigated Knowledge Management within consulting firms, and published their results in a 1999 *Harvard Business Review* paper. Knowledge Management is very important to consulting firms, where knowledge is the core (and some would say the only) asset. They argued that there were two very different Knowledge Management strategies, Codification and Personalisation:

1. Codification

In some companies (for example Ernst & Young and Andersen Consulting[3]) knowledge is carefully codified and stored on databases, where it can be accessed and used by anyone within the company as required. This requires a high dependence on IT systems such as document readers, and the discipline to input the knowledge generated by each and every consulting engagement. This allows the organisation to utilise a knowledge asset many times, with associated economies of scale (once the initial investment in IT is made). These companies can also use a graduate workforce well suited to the reuse of knowledge and the implementation of solutions without the need for a high level of input from partners, further reducing costs.

2. Personalisation

In other companies (for example McKinsey & Company and Bain & Company) knowledge is closely tied to the person who developed it and is shared mainly through interpersonal contact. The primary role of IT systems is to facilitate the sharing of this information, not the storing of it. This allows the organisation to provide creative, analytically rigorous advice on high level strategic problems by channelling individual expertise. However, this is at the cost of higher overheads, for example by requiring a higher level of partner input, and employing expensive MBAs rather than mere graduates. These overheads need to be offset by undertaking higher value assignments (or put another way, higher fees).

This paper very clearly favours personalisation as the superior method. It argues that it can be very difficult to codify Tacit Knowledge and retain the subtle detail and nuances found in face-to-face communication. The example of Xerox[4] is cited, which attempted to capture all the knowledge of their service and repair technicians in a database. However, this system reduced the time that the technicians spent together sharing stories and tips on how they had fixed problems with the machines, reducing their overall effectiveness. It should also be noted that one of the authors, Thomas Tierney, was the Managing Director of Bain & Company, so it is perhaps hardly surprising that the paper favours the Personalisation system employed by Bain!

Nevertheless, the difficulty of codifying Tacit Knowledge is not to be underestimated, especially as according to Professor Robert Grant the individual is the primary actor as both knowledge creator and the repository of knowledge. This has profound implications for organisations; if the source of your competitive advantage is knowledge, then what is to stop it simply walking out the door? The answer is to focus on developing an organisational culture that engages and motivates employees by supporting both Knowledge Management and innovation. How can this be achieved in practice? According to Adam Brand from 3M,[5] there are several factors that need to be combined:

1. **Clear Objectives and Goals**

   3M's objective is to become the most innovative company in the world. To be innovative in highly competitive industries and global markets requires the effective use of Knowledge Management, and 3M requires each of its businesses to deliver at least 30% of sales from products that did not exist four years ago. So, everyone at 3M knows what the overall objective is, how innovation and knowledge are linked, and what the goals relating to knowledge and innovation are.

2. Long Term Commitment & Continuity

Top managers at 3M see one of their major duties as facilitating knowledge sharing and innovation. Promotions are often from within, meaning people build up an in-depth understanding of the business and a strong network. Redundancy programmes are avoided, as are short-term contracts as these can damage loyalty and commitment to share knowledge and innovate.

3. Stories & Traditions

New employees quickly adsorb the company's stories and traditions. These reinforce the values and atmosphere that encourage information sharing and innovation. Somewhat counter-intuitively 3M stories often centre on employees who disregard management and continue to develop products that they believe in, for example Dick Drew's development of Scotch Tape in the 1920s. The company has a relatively high tolerance for mistakes, to encourage staff to experiment, make decisions and take some risks.

4. Recruitment & Retention

3M looks for people who want to start new things, rather than run the existing business. They are action orientated, self-motivated, have a multidisciplinary approach and are keen to network and learn new skills. Retaining such people requires developing an environment in which they can flourish, for example by the provision of...

5. ...Time, Funding and Recognition

3M has a '15% rule' which states that staff can spend 15% of their time working on innovative ideas of their own choosing.[6] The message is clear; it's OK to try something not on the main line. As well as time, 3M provides small grants to develop new technical ideas, for example buying specialist equipment. The company also has a dual promotion system, where non-management specialists can progress to Vice-President level on the basis of their technical contribution. There are also a number of award programmes in recognition of innovation.

It's worth remembering that this is not a rigid prescription; what works at 3M may not be appropriate for other organisations. However, the interlinking of knowledge management and innovation, facilitated by the right organisational culture, seems to have paid dividends at 3M.

SUGGESTED READING:

- **Blackler, F.** (1995). Knowledge, Knowledge Work and Organizations: An Overview and Interpretation, *Organization Studies*, 16(60), pp. 1021–1046.

- **Brand, A.** (1998). Knowledge Management and Innovation at 3M, *Journal of Knowledge Management*, 2(1), pp. 17–22.

- **Grant, R.M.** (1996). Towards a Knowledge Based Theory of the Firm, *Strategic Management Journal*, Winter Special Issue, pp. 109–122.

- **Hansen, M., Nohria, N. and Tierney, T.** (1999). What's Your Strategy for Managing Knowledge? *Harvard Business Review*, 77(2), pp. 106–116.

K: KNOWLEDGE MANAGEMENT

- **Plessis, M.** (2007). The Role of Knowledge Management in Innovation, *Journal of Knowledge Management*, 55(6), pp. 49–57.

- **Zack, M.H.** (1999). Developing a Knowledge Strategy, *California Management Journal*, 5, pp. 125–145.

NOTES:

1. Yes, this is the same Peter Drucker whose work we discussed in the section on Ideation (new knowledge being one of Drucker's sources of innovation). Hopefully by now you are recognising that these 26 Innovation Management themes do not exist in isolation, and that there is significant overlap between some of the key concepts.

2. The fact that you are reading this book makes it highly likely that you are already (or are about to become) a *Knowledge Worker* – earning your living from what you know and how you can apply and develop your knowledge.

3. Anderson Consulting originated as the consulting wing of the accounting firm Arthur Anderson, before becoming a separate business unit and then splitting entirely and renaming itself Accenture plc in 2001. The timing of the split was fortunate as Arthur Anderson became mired in the Enron scandal and eventually broke up.

4. We have an entire section on Xerox later in the book, happily (for me) filling the 'X' slot.

5. In brief, 3M formed in Minnesota in 1902 and has since become a multinational corporation employing over 80,000 people and producing over 50,000 products including adhesives, abrasives electronic materials, medical materials and car care products such as polish and wax. The diversity of its product range makes it a

frequent case study for Innovation Management. There is no truth to the rumour that employees say that 3M stands for 'meetings and more meetings'.

6. The '15% rule' has since been adopted by other firms, most notably Google. Interestingly, I can remember consulting for a global healthcare organisation where the sponsoring manager complained to me that his technical staff kept on requesting 15% 'playtime'. I asked if he would be happy if his technical staff asked to spend 15% of their time working on high value innovation projects. "Oh yes, that would be great!" came the reply. Moral of the story – if you want to successfully persuade your manager, make sure you frame your request in the right language.

Life Cycle

L: LIFE CYCLE

Products (and by extension technologies) have their own distinct Life Cycle, typically presented as a plot of annual market revenues against time. At the start of the product Life Cycle a new technology fights for market acceptance, before (hopefully) experiencing a growth phase, then maturity, decline, and finally obsolescence as it is replaced by another technology that offers the market greater utility (which could be superior functionality, lower price, or both). A good example from earlier in the book is vinyl records being superseded by compact discs, which in turn are being replaced by internet downloads.

Managing product Life Cycles presents a significant challenge to organisations. For example, the capabilities required to develop and launch a new product are significantly different from those required to maintain high sales in a mature market. And how do you effectively manage a declining market while ensuring that you are devoting sufficient resources to developing your own replacement technology? Fortunately there is a man who has spent the last 25 years carefully considering these questions, and his name is Geoff Moore.

Moore is an innovation consultant based in Silicon Valley, and has had ample opportunity to observe the birth, rise, and fall of many products, technologies and even companies. In Moore's view, investments in innovation have four potential returns:

1. **Differentiation**

   Innovation that delivers differentiation[1] in the marketplace allows the organisation to gain market share and charge higher prices than competitors.

2. **Neutralisation**

   Innovation that delivers neutralisation allows the organisation to catch up with a competitor's differentiated offering or meet a new market standard, thereby protecting market share.

3. Productivity

Innovation that delivers an increase in productivity reduces the organisation's costs, enabling it to achieve higher profit margins or higher market share by reducing prices. It can also free up resources that can then be redeployed to support Differentiation or Neutralisation programmes.

4. Waste

Some Differentiation, Neutralisation and Productivity innovation programmes will not succeed. This is never a good result, but some failure is to be expected – there is no such thing as risk-free innovation. However, Moore classifies as 'Waste' innovation programmes that go beyond what is required to succeed, but the additional investment yields no further returns. Similarly, Waste includes innovation programmes that achieve their stated objectives, but these are not enough to achieve a return; they were simply not ambitious enough.

Moore's great insight is that companies should carefully align their innovation strategy to fit specific segments of the Life Cycle, which are in turn aligned to the specific needs of the customer types identified by Everett Rogers's work on the diffusion of innovations (see the earlier section on Early Adopters). Moore proposes eight distinct phases within the Life Cycle:

1. Early Market

This is where a new technology is first introduced to the market. The customers who are attracted are the Innovators and then Early Adopters, but the technology is still perceived as risky by the rest of the market. During this phase, companies entering the market are best served with a Disruptive Innovation strategy that focuses on further developing the technology.

2. **The Chasm**

The technology has now been in the market for some time, and has lost some of its novelty. However, its acceptance is not yet widespread and it still has not convinced the Early Majority to adopt. To jump the 'Chasm' across to the main market, firms tend to focus on serving a very specific market niche where the technology is the sole solution to a particular problem. The classic example is the transistor, a technology which found a niche in portable radios.[2]

3. **Bowling Alley**

The technology is successful in its niche, and now begins to be accepted in adjacent niches (hence the bowling alley metaphor), where it builds up a loyal following. Vendors utilise an Application Innovation strategy to explore applications in additional market niches.

4. **Tornado**

The technology has now gained wider acceptance and is seen as necessary and standard for many applications, heralding a short period of intensive growth. New companies enter the market and revenue growth is double or even triple digit, attracting additional investors. Firms focus on a Product Innovation strategy where the aim is to steadily improve the functionality and performance of the technology.

5. Main Street (Early)

Intensive growth has started to transition into a new phase of steady long term growth as markets expand. Market leaders have emerged, although smaller companies are still performing well as the Early Majority starts to adopt the technology. Vendors focus on a Process Innovation strategy to streamline production, the supply chain and order fulfilment processes.

6. Main Street (Mature)

Growth in the market has now plateaued as the technology is increasingly seen as a commodity, though still useful. The market consolidates through mergers and acquisitions and the Late Majority start to adopt the technology. Vendors focus on Experiential and Marketing Innovation strategies. These improve customer's experience of using the technology and improve marketing communications and customer touch points.

7. Main Street (Declining)

The technology is now fully commoditised and some customers are actively looking for alternatives. The market is in need of disruption and a next generation of technology is on the horizon. Nevertheless, the declining market is still profitable, and Laggards are now adopting. Vendors focus on a Business Model Innovation[3] strategy to reframe the value proposition for customers. An example of this would be moving from a purchase and service model to an all-inclusive leasing model.

8. Fault Line and End of Life

The technology is now obsolete, with a clear Fault Line between what the market now wants and what the technology delivers.

> The next generation of technology is now being adopted, disrupting established vendors. There is no long term future for vendors that only produce an obsolete technology, although there may be a few Laggards willing to continue buying at rock bottom prices. Vendors now focus on a Structural Innovation strategy to completely reposition themselves in the market. An example would be IBM, who when facing Bankruptcy in the 1990s repositioned from hardware supplier to services provider.[4]

Of course, you may reasonably argue that if a company has allowed itself to progress all the way to the End of Life without any back-up plan other than 'Structural Innovation' then it hasn't done a particularly good job at managing itself. For example, it could have improved its situation by having a portfolio of different technologies, all at different points in the Life Cycle. But this approach depends on being able to redeploy resource from the day-to-day profit generating activities that support a mature market to risky and speculative front-end innovation. This is often a tricky thing to do, as explored in the earlier sections on Ambidexterity and Horizons.

Moore acknowledges this issue and suggests that organisations review their activities and categorise them as either Core or Context.

He defines Core as:

> 'Any activity that creates sustainable differentiation in the target market, resulting in premium prices or increased sales'

Companies investing in developing the Core seek to dramatically outperform all competitors within the domain of the core. In contrast, Context is defined as:

> 'Any activity that does not differentiate the company from the customer's viewpoint in the target market'

That isn't to say that Context activities are non-value added or unimportant. Moore makes a further distinction between Mission Critical and Non-Mission Critical. Mission Critical Context activities would include areas such as Finance. An absence of rigorous financial control would hazard the organisation. However, performing financial management better than competitors is not valued by customers.

Non-Mission Critical Context activities are those that can be easily outsourced. These could include manufacturing, warehousing, transportation and some administrative functions. It is the outsourcing of Non-Mission Critical context activities that provides the resource[5] to invest in developing core activities.

Does any of this theory actually work in practice? Well, Innovation Management at networking giant Cisco has been heavily influenced by Moore's work, with CEO John Chambers acknowledging his contribution. And I can recall attending an Innovation conference in London where the Chief Technology Officer of Unilever outlined their innovation strategy. About five minutes into it I realised that it was all based on Moore's models! Terms such as 'Chasm', 'Tornado' and 'Fault Line' have all entered the lexicon of Innovation Management, and the selection of his works highlighted below are well worth exploring.

SUGGESTED READING:

- **Moore, G.** (1991). *Crossing the Chasm: Marketing and Selling High-Tech Products to Mainstream Customers*, New York: Harper Business.

- **Moore, G.** (2004). Darwin and the Demon: Innovating Within Established Enterprises, *Harvard Business Review*, July, pp. 87–92.

- **Moore, G.** (2006). *Dealing with Darwin: How Great Companies Innovate at Every Phase of Their Evolution*, Chichester: Wiley.

L: LIFE CYCLE

NOTES:

1. Differentiation is an important concept in the field of Strategic Management. According to Harvard Professor Michael Porter (who we came across earlier in the section on Clusters) companies can achieve a sustained competitive advantage over their rivals by three generic strategies. The first is differentiation, where customers pay a price premium for a product or service that they cannot obtain from other companies. The second is cost leadership, where customers simply select the lowest cost vendor, who sacrifices profit margins for high market share. The third is a niche strategy, where a company aligns their offering to exactly meet the needs of a specific niche market that they go on to dominate.

2. The transistor was developed by AT&T's Bell labs in the 1940s as a semiconductor device that amplifies and switches electrical signals and power. Transistors were small, required low power, and were reliable; all significant improvements over existing vacuum tube technology. The first application niche for transistors came from portable radios, with Japanese start-up Sony quickly becoming the market leader. From this success transistors were rapidly adopted, becoming a fundamental component of modern electronic devices.

3. However, it could be argued that waiting for the market to start declining before considering business model innovation is a mistake. Combing product and process innovation earlier in the Life Cycle with business model innovation could generate an overall value proposition that is far superior to rivals.

4. An engaging account of IBM's transformation can be found in former CEO Louis Gerstner's (somewhat immodestly titled) 2002 book *Who Says Elephants Can't Dance?: How I turned around IBM.*

5. Of course, Moore is not saying that you can simply redeploy outsourced Human Resources administrators to the New Products Division and demand that they start innovating. It is the overall saving of resource that needs to be redeployed to developing the core of the business, which may require new hires. Too often organisations simply bank the cash saved from outsourcing without reinvesting. This may please the Director of Finance, but is unlikely to generate future growth.

Management Innovation

M: MANAGEMENT INNOVATION

Up to this point we have generally framed innovation outputs in terms of either new 'products' (for example an iPod) or new 'services' (for example iTunes). However, some researchers argue that the really big pay-off from innovation comes not from new products or services in themselves, but by focusing attention on how to develop new ways of managing organisations, or Management Innovation. Perhaps the most vocal champion of Management Innovation is Professor Gary Hamel,[1] who provides the following definition:

> 'Management Innovation is a marked departure from traditional management principles, processes, and practices or a departure from customary organisational forms that significantly alters the way the work of management is performed'

What activities do managers currently perform? In my experience the list includes such items as:

- Making phone calls, sending emails, arranging meetings.
- Receiving phone calls, reading emails, attending meetings.
- Setting goals, objectives and planning activities.
- Controlling resources, budgeting, hiring and firing.
- Motivating employees, identifying and developing new talent.
- Communicating and coordinating with internal interfaces, for example functional departments, business units, and the board of directors.
- Communicating and coordinating with external interfaces, for example customers, suppliers, shareholders and government.

All worthy enough, but will they necessarily lead to a breakthrough in organisational performance? Probably not. One of the main problems with management is that it is easy to get caught up in day-to-day issues, and never dedicating the time to think strategically. However, Hamel cites several examples of organisations that have reaped the rewards of introducing radically different management techniques, including:

- **General Electric**

  General Electric developed the first industrial scale R&D capability in the early 1900s. This innovation brought management discipline to the process of scientific discovery, leading to the granting of more patents than any other US company over the next 50 years. GE has extended this approach to systematically developing exceptional leaders, for example by training at its purpose built Crotonville educational facility, implementing 360 degree feedback, and rigorously measuring management performance (and firing the bottom 10%).

- **Proctor & Gamble**

  Proctor & Gamble developed the first formalised approach to brand management in the 1930s. This allowed the company to steadily develop a diverse product portfolio with enhanced value through the intangible asset of brands such as Tide detergent, Crest toothpaste, Gillette razors, Olay skin care and (my favourite) Pringles crisps. Today, P&G are one of the first major adopters of the Open Innovation[2] model of developing external links to provide access to new technologies and market opportunities.

- **General Motors**

  General Motors is credited with developing the divisionalised organisational structure in response to the problem of how to effectively manage the vast family of companies and products that had evolved since its formation. The new structure, designed by Alfred P. Sloan in the 1930s, established a centralised executive committee that set policy and exercised financial control alongside operating divisions organised by product and responsible for day-to-day operations.

- **Toyota**

  Toyota has been able to take a significant market share from US rivals by producing low cost, high quality and reliable cars. But behind this formula is their capability to drive continuous improvement by giving production line employees the skills, tools and permission to solve problems as they arise and to head off new problems before they occur. This system is in marked contrast to the US system of expecting employees to be little more than unthinking cogs in an automated production line.[3]

According to Hamel, the foundation of Management Innovation is to purposely and systematically focus on identifying and solving a big management problem. The bigger the problem, the bigger the opportunity to generate a breakthrough that leads to a significant competitive advantage. To do this organisations should ask three simple but searching questions:

1. **What are your current trade-offs?**

   Business and management is full of trade-offs such as quality versus cost; standardisation versus customisation; make versus buy; consolidation versus expansion; simplicity versus complexity; focus versus diversification. Management Innovation is often driven by the desire to break these types of trade-off. For example, open source software development requires the combination of two seemingly incompatible ideas; radical decentralisation with disciplined large scale project management. And as previously highlighted, Toyota produced high quality at low cost through the innovation of continuous improvement.

2. **What is your organisation bad at?**

Ouch! If you are being honest then this should produce a pretty long list. This can include resistance to change, inability to spot market shifts, poor implementation of improvement projects (particularly if the project involves IT), and failure to fully tap into the energy and creativity of employees. However, these problems are your opportunity to develop radical solutions through Management Innovation.

3. **What are your emerging challenges?**

If you thought addressing your current organisational deficiencies was tough then try looking into the future at your emerging challenges; ever-accelerating technological change, rapidly increasing customer power, low-cost competitors and new market entrants, even social and political resistance and cynicism regarding 'big business'. These discontinuities will demand that organisations develop Management Innovation capabilities in order to remain competitive.

What can managers do to improve their organisation's capacity for Management Innovation? This is a question asked by London Business School Professors Julian Birkinshaw and Michael Mol in their 2006 MIT *Sloan Management Review* paper (written with the support of Gary Hamel). They suggest four key areas to develop:

M: MANAGEMENT INNOVATION

1. Create a questioning and problem solving culture

Developing Management Innovation relies on engaging all of the organisation's employees to focus on overcoming unusual management problems or challenges. It's not just a top-down directive. If you don't already have a questioning and problem solving culture then congratulations, developing one is your first Management Innovation challenge!

2. Identify analogies and exemplars from different environments

Exposing employees to different types of environment can help provide the insights required to solve management problems. For example, if a commercial organisation wants to improve employee motivation and engagement then studying the not-for-profit sector, open source software development, or sports teams can provide analogies and exemplars that enable innovative solutions to be developed.

3. Build a capacity for low-risk experimentation

It would be a mistake to attempt a full scale launch of multiple Management Innovation programmes across an organisation. This may lead to confusion and even organisational paralysis. Instead, organisations should aim to develop an experimental model where ideas can be tested on a small scale for a limited period of time before evaluation. Only once an idea has been shown to deliver business benefits should it be rolled out. In order for an experimental model to work the funding for small scale trials needs to be made available, as well securing senior management project sponsorship.

4. Use external change agents to explore new idea

According to Birkinshaw and Mol, there is value in selectively making use of academics and consultants in developing Management Innovation. Speaking as an academic and consultant myself, they are undoubtedly correct! External agents can represent a source of new ideas from different environments, act as a sounding board for management innovation development, and help evaluate and validate Management Innovation programme outcomes.

SUGGESTED READING:

- **Birkinshaw, J. and Mol, M.** (2006). How Management Innovation Happens, *MIT Sloan Management Review,* 47(4), pp. 81–88.
- **Birkinshaw, J., Hamel, G. and Mol, M.** (2008). Management Innovation, *Academy of Management Review*, 33(4), pp. 825–845.
- **Hamel, G.** (2006). The Why, What, and How of Management Innovation, *Harvard Business Review*, 84(2), pp. 72–84.

NOTES:

1. Professor Gary Hamel is probably best known for his work on developing the 'Resource Based View' of strategy in the 1990s (together with the late C.K. Prahalad). His more recent work has focused on developing competencies in innovation, and the exploring the relationship between innovation and strategy.
2. We'll cover Open Innovation in detail later on in the book. For additional insights into innovation at P&G I recommend Bruce Brown and Scott Anthony's 2011 *Harvard Business Review* article 'How P&G tripled its innovation success rate'.

3. Of course, Henry Ford's development of the Production Line for the Model T can be considered a significant innovation in its own right, simultaneously increasing production output rate and reducing unit cost. Ford also decided to pay his workers an industry-leading $5 a day. Why pay so much for repetitive manual work where employees could be easily replaced? Well, the industry suffered from high employee turnover and poor labour relations. By paying top dollar workers stayed with Ford, reducing turnover and the associated hiring, retraining, and disruption costs. As discussed in the section on Disruptive Innovation paying workers $5 a day also ensured that they could afford to buy a Model T, rapidly expanding sales.

Not-Invented-Here Syndrome

N: NOT-INVENTED-HERE SYNDROME

If you think that Not-Invented-Here Syndrome sounds like some sort of dreadful innovation killing organisational disease then you're not far wrong. Perhaps the most well-known example of N.I.H. syndrome concerns the British inventor and entrepreneur James Dyson. In the late 1970s, after years of experimentation, Dyson achieved a breakthrough in vacuum cleaner performance with his dual cyclone constant suction technology. His plan was to licence the technology to existing vacuum cleaner manufacturers such as Hoover and Electrolux and then have a well-earned break as the royalty fees rolled in. But despite his confidence in the utility of his technology, one-by-one he was rejected by the established firms – classic N.I.H. Syndrome.

Suitably annoyed, Dyson started his own manufacturing operations and quickly succeeded in becoming the market leader in the UK, and also became the market leader in the USA and Japan (the world's largest and third largest economies). At the time of writing his company employs over 3,000 people and has developed a wide portfolio of consumer products. As for Dyson himself, he now has a net worth of some £3 billion. Not bad for a guy whose only previous notable success was the invention of the Ball-Barrow (look it up…). The story of Dyson has in many ways become a modern day parable on innovation, and one thing is for sure; if Hoover could turn back the clock they would have licensed Dyson's technology.

The first academic study into N.I.H. Syndrome was made back in 1967 by Robert Clagett, a hardworking (I assume…) masters student at Massachusetts Institute of Technology, with his thesis entitled 'Receptivity to Innovation – Overcoming N.I.H'. Clagett studied eight cases of successful and unsuccessful implementations of process innovations developed in the R&D unit of a large US based firm. He observed that the acronym 'N.I.H.' had been used by staff to describe the attitude of technical organisations that resist the adoption of innovations proposed from sources outside of the organisation.

Fifteen years later the study of N.I.H. was revived by professors Ralph Katz and Thomas Allen who introduced the phrase 'Not-Invented-Here Syndrome' and proposed the now widely accepted definition as:

> 'The tendency of a project group of stable composition to believe it possesses a monopoly of knowledge in its field which leads it to reject ideas from outsiders, to the likely detriment of its performance.'

Of course, if you have already read the section on Knowledge Management you will appreciate why the persistent rejection of ideas, knowledge or technologies from outside of the organisation is a serious mistake. As the economies of the developed world continue to be driven by knowledge, organisations must increasingly look for external sources of ideas, knowledge and technology to complement their internal capabilities. To fail to do this puts the organisation at a significant competitive disadvantage, leading to eventual failure if the situation persists.

However, the particularly dangerous aspect of Not-Invented-Here Syndrome is that it often occurs at the subconscious level of decision making. This can make it difficult to diagnose and cure (to continue with the medical themed terminology). There are several explanations for why this may happen:

- General organisational resistance to any change in the familiar working environment which may cause additional levels of uncertainty or effort.

- Resistance to external technology due to the potential damage to the organisation's collective identity (for example "We are the leaders in Technology X, why do we need outsiders?").

- A subconscious desire to reduce stress and insecurity in the working environment leads to routines and rigid roles in stable project teams which reduce the openness to external ideas, knowledge and technology.

- Reward and incentive schemes which only encourage the development of internally generated ideas, knowledge and technology.
- Historical negative experiences with externally generated ideas, knowledge or technology leading to an overly cautious and sceptical mindset.
- External ideas, knowledge and technology are perceived as inherently higher risk than those generated internally and therefore are not pursued.
- External ideas, knowledge and technology are perceived as a threat to status and job security, particularly within the science, engineering, technology and R&D communities.
- Generally poor innovation strategy and leadership within the organisation leads to a lack of awareness of the benefits of seeking out external sources of ideas, knowledge and technology.

A major development in extending the field came in 1990 with the publication of Wesley Cohen and Daniel Levinthal's seminal paper 'Absorptive Capacity: A New Perspective on Learning and Innovation'. Absorptive Capacity (which narrowly missed out on being the *'A'* for this book) is defined as:

> 'The ability of a firm to recognise the value of new, external information, assimilate it, and apply it to commercial ends'

Importantly, Cohen and Levinthal argue that the firm's existing level of knowledge (which may come from R&D or manufacturing expertise) underpins its ability to absorb external knowledge. So in this respect external knowledge cannot be used to fully substitute internal knowledge, but is instead complementary.

Clearly a firm's overall absorptive capacity will be strongly related to the absorptive capacity of its individual members, and so careful consideration of employee recruitment and development policy is required. However, there are other steps that can be taken to enhance organisational absorptive capacity and reduce the influence of Not-Invented-Here Syndrome. These include:

- Ensuring that project teams are regularly refreshed. Katz and Allen suggest that three years is about right, and that Not-Invented-Here Syndrome can start to take hold after this point is reached.

- Ensuring that internal knowledge generating capability, for example R&D, remains strong in order to be able to effectively assimilate external knowledge.

- Paying close attention to communication systems and Boundary Spanning roles to ensure that knowledge diffuses across organisational interfaces.

- Fostering a culture of continuous learning within the organisation through the development of problem solving skills and capturing the lessons of past successes and failures.

- Recognising, rewarding, and publicising successful projects that utilise both internal and external knowledge in order to reinforce the right organisational behaviours.

So in summary, organisations should aim to avoid Not-Invented-Here Syndrome and increase their absorptive capacity in order to capitalise on external sources of ideas, knowledge, and technology. But, as the TV detective Columbo would say, "There's just one more thing..."

There is perhaps a danger that in the quest to avoid Not-Invented-Here Syndrome organisations can become seduced into overestimating the value of external knowledge. In Karl Laden's fantastically titled (and admirably short) 1996 paper 'Not Invented There, or, the Other Person's Dessert Always Looks Better!' he introduces the concept of Buy-In Syndrome. This is like the evil twin of N.I.H. Syndrome, and is defined as:

> 'An attitude to the external acquisition of knowledge that is more positive than the ideal economic attitude would be'

Buy-in Syndrome is often caused by a lack in confidence in the organisation's own abilities, and can be further exacerbated by exaggerated claims by the external knowledge source organisation, particularly if they have a strong reputation in the market. If allowed to go unchecked Buy-in Syndrome can have serious consequences for the organisation.

These include draining cash reserves unnecessarily, a lack of investment in internal capabilities, an over-reliance on external companies, and an undifferentiated position in the market place – which would definitely not meet the approval of strategist Michael Porter.

So, the lesson is that managers need to take a balanced view on what external knowledge to acquire, how much to pay for it, and what to develop internally.

SUGGESTED READING:

- **Clagett, R.P.** (1967). *Receptivity to Innovation – Overcoming N.I.H.*, Masters Thesis, Boston MA: MIT.
- **Cohen, W. and Levinthal, D.** (1990). Absorptive Capacity: A New Perspective on Learning and Innovation, *Administrative Science Quarterly*, 35, pp. 128–32.

N: NOT-INVENTED-HERE SYNDROME

- **Katz, R. and Allen, T.** (1982). Investigating the Not Invented Here (NIH) Syndrome: A Look at the Performance, Tenure, and Communication Patterns of 50 R&D Project Groups, *R&D Management*, 12(1), pp. 7–19.

- **Laden, K.** (1996). Not Invented There, or, the Other Persons Dessert Always Looks Better!, *Research Technology Management*, 39, pp. 10–12.

- **Lichtenthaler, U. and Ernst, H.** (2006). Attitudes to Externally Organising Knowledge Management Tasks: A Review, Reconsideration and Extension of the NIH Syndrome, *R&D Management*, 36(4), pp. 367–386.

- **Menon, T. and Pfeffer, J.** (2003). Valuing Internal vs. External Knowledge: Explaining the Preference for Outsiders, *Management Science*, 49, pp. 497–513.

- **Zahra, M. and George, G.** (2002). Absorptive Capacity: A Review, Reconceptualization, and Extension, *Academy of Management Review*, 27, pp. 185–203.

Open Innovation

O: OPEN INNOVATION

It is somewhat ironic that this section immediately follows the section on Not-Invented-Here Syndrome! The term Open Innovation was coined by Berkley academic Professor Henry Chesbrough in his 2002 book *Open Innovation: The new imperative for creating and profiting from technology*. It is based on the view that valuable ideas and knowledge can come from outside of a company, as well as from internal sources such as traditional R&D departments. A good example of this view is found in the 2000 Annual Report from the pharmaceutical giant Merck, which states:

> 'Merck accounts for about 1% of the biomedical research in the world. To tap into the remaining 99%, we must actively reach out to universities, research institutions and companies worldwide to bring the best technology and potential products into Merck. The cascade of knowledge flowing from biotechnology and the unravelling of the human genome – to name only two recent developments – is far too complex for any one company to handle alone.'

The issue of increased complexity across technology-based sectors is one of the key drivers for seeking external ideas and knowledge. According to Chesbrough, the 20th century model of vertically integrated companies with large internal R&D centres driving new product development has slowly given way to more collaborative and cost-effective ways of conducting research. Ever more specialised technology combined with the availability of private equity funding and flexible labour markets has seen the growth of small start-up companies which are now conducting an increasing amount of research. This is in contrast to an overall decrease in the amount of research conducted by larger companies.[1]

However, many would argue that external collaborations have always been sought by large research intensive companies. For example, since 1990 the UK engineering group Rolls-Royce plc has formed around 30 formal collaborations with leading universities around the world. As far ago as 1988, Professor Eric von Hippel identified seven sources of useful external knowledge used by companies: suppliers; customers; universities; government research laboratories; private research laboratories; competitors (whose innovations can be imitated); and knowledge from other nations. Some have (somewhat harshly) criticised Open Innovation as just 'old wine in new bottles'.

So, what is 'new' about Open Innovation, and how does it represent a new paradigm in innovation strategy? Chesbrough argues that there are eight features of Open Innovation which make it distinctive from previous models of collaborative innovation:

1. **Open Innovation is underpinned by a robust business model**

   A fundamental characteristic of Open Innovation is that value creation and value capture are driven by a robust business model designed to exploit the benefits of external ideas and knowledge. For many companies ideas and knowledge drawn from external sources are just adsorbed into the R&D department.

   Furthermore, the work conducted in traditional R&D departments is often only loosely tied to the company's business strategy. Companies that are successfully utilising Open Innovation have specifically changed their business model in order to maximise the benefits of external collaborations. For these companies Open Innovation is fully integrated into their business model, not just a 'bolt-on' which makes a small contribution to competitiveness.

2. **External ideas and knowledge are viewed as equal in value to internally generated ideas and knowledge**

   Companies that embrace Open Innovation view ideas and knowledge from external sources as equal in value to internally generated ideas and knowledge. These companies have overcome the widespread Not-Invented-Here Syndrome in which external ideas and knowledge are viewed as low quality and inherently risky. Even if a company does engage with external collaborations, the benefits of these collaborations are likely to be severely restricted without first overcoming N.I.H. Syndrome.

3. External ideas and knowledge are viewed as abundant

Traditional R&D intensive companies believe that ideas and knowledge are a scarce resource, and trying to find what you are looking for outside of the company is like looking for a needle in a haystack. Far better to focus on internal resources, because there is more chance of eventually generating what it is that you are looking for.

In contrast, companies that have successfully embraced Open Innovation not only believe that external ideas and knowledge are of equal value to internally generated ideas and knowledge, but that they are also abundant and widely distributed. These companies therefore invest the time and resources to track down these external sources.

4. Outbound technology flows open up new markets

Traditional R&D-intensive firms seek external ideas and knowledge to supplement internal development, manufacture, and sales. Companies adopting an Open Innovation business model utilise external ideas and knowledge to open up new markets for their existing technologies – particularly technologies which have not yet found a route to market. In this way external ideas and knowledge become market enablers, allowing companies to make larger returns on their technology investments.

5. Proactive Intellectual Property (IP) management

Traditional R&D intensive companies employ IP protection, particularly through Patents[2]. By creating a temporary monopoly through patenting these companies aim to create a window of opportunity to develop new products, while preventing their competitors from developing similar products. However, patenting IP is expensive, and does not guarantee market success.

Companies utilising an Open Innovation strategy are much more proactive in extracting the latent value from their intellectual property. For example selling IP, licensing deals, and even sharing, donating or publishing IP is employed if it will release future value.

6. Technology intermediaries are utilised

Companies adopting an Open Innovation strategy recognise the ever increasing complexity of technology, and the rapid pace of change. For these reasons they are likely to employ technology intermediaries to facilitate access to external ideas and knowledge. This is a particular trend in the pharmaceuticals sector, but growing across other sectors through intermediaries such as NineSigma and Innocentive.

7. Project evaluation focuses on making gains rather than avoiding losses

Many companies manage innovation as a process which utilises staged gates to filter R&D projects as they progress. These processes discard projects which do not fit the company's business model or strategic focus, or projects which carry high perceived levels of risk. This risk has three components:

- Will the technology actually work?
- Will there be a market for it?
- Will I get the blame if something goes wrong?

In this way the innovation process is set up to filter out so-called Type I Errors, also known as false positives i.e. projects which are expected to succeed but fail commercially.

However, companies that adopt an Open Innovation strategy are also concerned with Type II Errors, false negatives. These are projects which were predicted to fail (and therefore terminated) but in actual fact would have succeeded. These companies take a much stronger line on avoiding missed opportunities, rather than being predominantly focused on filtering out risk.

This distinction is particularly important when companies are aiming for radical innovation[3] rather than incremental innovation. Radical innovation inherently carries higher levels of risk, but with the opportunity for higher rewards. But by pushing radical innovations through a traditional risk reducing stage gate process it is almost inevitable that at some stage they will be terminated. By adopting an Open Innovation strategy which focuses on making gains rather than avoiding losses it is more likely that radical innovations will succeed.

8. Different metrics are used to measure Open Innovation

The final aspect which distinguishes Open Innovation as a new innovation model is the use of a different set of metrics to measure success. Traditional inwardly looking measures of innovation include:

- R&D spend as a percentage of sales.
- Number of patents as a percentage of R&D spend.
- Number of R&D employees.
- Percentage of 'new' products taken to market.

These metrics will still be important, but a new set of metrics will also be needed to manage Open Innovation, for example:

- Percentage of R&D conducted external to the firm (for example, in the supply chain).
- Rate of patent utilisation and income from technology licencing.
- Number of employees dedicated to external networks.
- Number of external networks and channels to market.

Overall, there is no doubt that the concept of Open Innovation has captured the imagination of both the research community and practitioners. I was fortunate to recently attend a keynote by Henry Chesbrough at a conference in Barcelona,[4] where he made a convincing case for Open Innovation and its increased adoption. He noted that before his book a Google search for the keywords 'Open' and 'Innovation' yielded a handful of results, usually concerning companies that had opened a centre for innovation. A Google search now gives 80 million results!

O: OPEN INNOVATION

SUGGESTED READING:

- **Chesbrough, H.** (2002). *Open Innovation; the new Imperative for Creating and Profiting from Technology*, Boston MA: Harvard Business School Press.

- **Chesbrough, H.** (2003). The Era of Open Innovation, *MIT Sloan Management Review*, 44(3), pp. 35–41.

- **Chesbrough, H.** (2007). Why companies should have open business models. *MIT Sloan Management Review*, 48(2), pp. 1–22.

- **Huston, L. and Sakkab, N.** (2006). Connect and Develop: Inside P&Gs New Model for Innovation, *Harvard Business Review*, 84(3), pp. 58–66.

- **Lichtenthaler, U.** (2011). Open Innovation: Past Research, Current Debates, and Future Directions, *Academy of Management Perspectives*, 25(1), pp. 75–93.

- **Trott, P. and Hartmann, D.** (2009). Why 'Open Innovation' is Old Wine in New Bottles, *International Journal of Innovation Management*, 13(4), pp. 715–736.

NOTES:

1. Chesbrough cites that in 1981 70% of all Industrial R&D in the US was undertaken by companies with more than 25,000 employees. But by 2001, this had fallen to less than 40% as the R&D output of smaller companies rose. One can infer that many of these small R&D intensive companies are likely to be the high growth Gazelles proposed by David Birch (see section G).

2. Somewhat helpfully, patents are the very next topic of the book. I didn't plan it this way, it's just how it worked out.

3. And Radical Innovation also makes it as a topic in its own right. Hopefully it's becoming clear that the innovation topics covered in this book do not exist in isolation, but are often interdependent and mutually reinforcing.

4. And in case you were wondering the answer is no, the fact that this conference was held in Barcelona had no bearing at all on my decision to attend, not even a tiny bit...

Patents

P: PATENTS

Innovation requires a significant investment in time and resources to create, develop and commercialise new technologies and products. In addition, firms must also accept the inherent risks associated with potential technological or market failure. However, the commercial rewards associated with successful innovation would be significantly reduced if competitors were free to launch their own copies into the market place, and this would be a disincentive for investment and risk taking by pioneers. An overall reduction of innovation activity in markets and the wider economy would clearly be an unsatisfactory situation, and therefore governments have developed a legal framework to protect the 'Intellectual Property' of pioneers, with Patents emerging as the strongest form of protection. Intellectual Property can be broadly thought of as:

> 'The ownership of intangible assets such as new ideas, concepts, names, designs and artistic works'

In addition to patents there are three other methods of legally protecting Intellectual Property; Copyright, Trademarks and Registered Designs.[1]

1. Copyright

Copyright is an automatic right that protects the authors of original work such as writing, music or art from unauthorised copying for up to 70 years after the originator's death. For example, this book is protected by copyright, so you can't make or distribute paper or electronic copies without breaking the law. Just thought I'd mention it...

2. Trademarks

Trademarks are words, logos, pictures, sounds, shapes, or a combination of these elements that indicate the origin of goods or services. Registering a trademark (for a fee) allows you to stop others using it without permission. Once granted trademarks must be renewed every ten years, but this can be done indefinitely.

3. Registered Designs

Registered designs protect the appearance of a product from being copied, in particular its lines, contours, shape and texture. The design must be new and deemed to have individual character, but once this is established the protection lasts for up to 25 years subject to the payment of registration and renewal fees.

In contrast to copyright, trademarks and registered designs the purpose of a patent is to protect the intellectual property that underpins products or processes that utilise new technologies or have new functionalities. If a patent is granted by the Intellectual Property Office (IPO) then it provides a temporary monopoly for the inventor in exchange for fully disclosing the invention.[2]

This monopoly is usually has a duration of 20 years (or 15 years for medicines and pharmaceuticals).[3] During this period the patent holder receives exclusive rights to exploit the invention by making and selling the product themselves, subcontracting manufacture and selling the product, licencing the patent rights in exchange for a royalty payment, or by simply selling the patent rights to a third party.[4] However, in order for a patent to be granted a new invention must pass three tests:

1. Novelty

The invention must be new and not previously disclosed to the public before the date the patent is applied for. This means that it is vital not to disclose the invention to anyone apart from to your legal representatives, such as a patent attorney. So, if you have a flash of inspiration, keep it to yourself until you have filed your patent application.

2. Inventiveness

The invention must not be obvious, or a minor modification or extension of what is already known. So, you can't patent a five legged chair or a laptop with 15 USB ports. Sorry.

3. Industrial Application

The invention must be deemed to make a positive technical contribution to industry, i.e. it must demonstrate its practical usefulness. So, no chocolate teapots please.

In addition to satisfying these tests there are also certain ideas that cannot be patented:

- Scientific or mathematical discoveries, theories or methods. So for example, Sir Isaac Newton couldn't have patented his Laws of Motion or Theory of Universal Gravity.
- Literary, dramatic, musical or artistic works (but these are automatically covered by copyright).
- Methods of doing business (unless technological innovation is involved).
- Methods of medical treatment, diagnosis or surgery. For example, you can patent a novel artificial artery, but not the surgical procedure required to fit it.
- Methods for presenting information and some computer programs.[5]
- Animal or plant varieties, for example a new breed of dairy cow or drought-resistant wheat.

- Anything which is deemed to be against public policy or morality, for example a new technology specifically designed to allow criminals to access personal information.

What are the disadvantages with patents? As stated above, monopoly rights are only granted for either 20 or 15 years, after which rivals can copy the invention, details of which are now fully disclosed and publicly available. Firms therefore need to ensure that they commercialise and monetise the invention successfully and establish a dominant market position within this period. This can be an issue for industries such as pharmaceuticals, where the time taken for additional medical trials and regulatory approval after a patent has been granted can delay the commercial launch of new drugs and treatments.

Patents can also be expensive and time consuming. The process usually requires the services of a highly paid patent attorney, it can take up to 4 years for a patent to be granted, and even then the patent will only cover the country of issue. Overseas or worldwide patent protection involves significant additional complexity and expenditure.

But perhaps the largest drawback of patents is that if the inventor feels that their patent has been infringed by a competitor then they must pursue this through the civil courts at their own expense, with no guarantee of their complaint being upheld. A well-known example of this concerns James Dyson, the British inventor of the dual cyclone vacuum cleaner we came across in the section on Not-Invented-Here Syndrome. Dyson was forced to defend a patent infringement by the American giant Hoover, eventually winning £4 million in damages and £2 million in costs. Of course, if Dyson had lost then he would have had to foot the legal bill himself, and possibly Hoover's as well. For these reasons many firms adopt alternative strategies to protect their intellectual property. These include:

P: PATENTS

1. Secrecy

Secrecy can be an effective form of protection when the production or functionality of the product requires information not generally known by competitors. 'Trade secrets' can be legally protected by non-disclosure agreements (NDAs), but these can often be rendered ineffective as staff move between different companies. In addition, many products can simply be 'reverse-engineered' by competitors.

2. Knowhow

Knowhow refers to the tacit knowledge required to get something done. Tacit knowledge is often firm specific, takes time to build up, and can be difficult to transfer or imitate. For example, the efficiency and high quality of the Toyota production line is underpinned by their tacit knowledge of how to engage and empower frontline employees to identify and solve problems.

3. The Learning Curve

As briefly discussed in the section on First Mover Advantage the Learning Curve is a concept popularised by the Boston Consulting Group in the 1970s. It proposes that unit costs decrease as production volume increases and the firm learns how to manufacture their product more efficiently. Pioneers will therefore enjoy a cost advantage over new entrants because they will be further advanced along the Learning Curve. This in turn means that they can offer customers lower prices than competitors and defend their market share.

4. Product Complexity

Some products have high levels of complexity which makes copying difficult, even if reverse-engineered. For example, you can take a gas turbine engine apart with a spanner and screwdriver, but that does not mean that you will gain sufficient understanding of the design, aerodynamic, thermodynamic, materials engineering, manufacturing engineering and regulatory requirements required to copy it.

5. Standardisation

The pioneer aims to become the standard in the market, locking out new entrants. This concept is explored in more detail in the section on QWERTY, which by sheer coincidence is the very next section.

In practice, most companies use a combination of legal and non-legal strategies to protect their intellectual property. Larger companies operating in technology-driven markets tend to place the patent at the heart of their intellectual property protection strategy, particularly if they undertake significant amounts of R&D. In fact, the annual number of patents applications filed is often used as a proxy to measure R&D effectiveness by both companies and policy makers (and in turn R&D effectiveness is often used as a proxy to measure innovation effectiveness, although in my view this is an over-simplistic metric).

Despite the limitations highlighted above, the patent system is still widely viewed as supporting and encouraging invention and innovation. However, could it be that the patent system may also act as a disincentive to invention and innovation? A recent phenomena that is attracting practitioner anxiety and academic interest is the emergence of so-called patent 'sharks' or 'trolls'. These are companies that hold large portfolios of patents with the specific aim of making money by aggressively extracting royalty payments and damage awards from firms that they accuse of infringing their patents.

According to a 2007 Research Policy paper by Markus Reitzig, Joachim Henkel and Christopher Heath these shark companies appear to be growing in both number and sophistication, ruthlessly pursuing their 'prey' through the courts. The emergence of patent sharks places additional costs on companies engaging in technological innovation through increased due diligence requirements and also the costs of fighting and settling a case if they become prey. It may also instil a heightened sense of caution and risk aversion, stifling innovation for fear of future litigation.

Sharks, of course, argue that they are operating within the law and are doing nothing wrong. It remains to be seen whether legislation regarding patents is modified to discourage the sharks, or whether they grow and continue to feed. What is clear is that the patent will remain the strongest form of intellectual property protection and continue to play a key role in the dynamics of innovation.

SUGGESTED READING:

- **Aggarwal, R.** (2010). Business Strategies for Multinational Intellectual Property Protection, *Thunderbird International Business Review*, 52(6), pp. 541–551.

- **Ananad, B. and Galetovic, A.** (2004). How Market Smarts Can Protect Property Rights, *Harvard Business Review*, December, pp. 73–79.

- **Arundel, A.** (2001). The Relative Effectiveness of Patents and Secrecy for Appropriation, *Research Policy*, 30(4), pp. 611–624.

P: PATENTS

- **Bainbridge, D.** (2012). *Intellectual Property*, 9th ed. London: Pearson.

- **Intellectual Property Office** (2014). *Patents: Essential Reading*, Cardiff: Intellectual Property Office.

- **Pisano, G. and Teece, D.** (2007). How to Capture Value from Innovation: Shaping Intellectual Property and Industry Architecture, *California Management Review*, 50(1), pp. 278–296.

- **Reitzig, M.** (2004). Strategic Management of Intellectual Property, *MIT Sloan Management Review*, 45(3), pp. 35–40.

- **Reitzig, M., Henkel, J. and Heath, C.** (2007). On Sharks, Trolls, and Their Patent Prey – Unrealistic Damage Awards and Firms' Strategies of 'Being Infringed', *Research Policy*, 36(1), pp. 134–154.

- **Rivette, K. and Kline, D.** (2000). *Rembrandts in the Attic: Unlocking the Hidden Value of Patents*, Boston MA: Harvard Business School Press.

NOTES:

1. It has to be emphasised that this section on patents and intellectual property protection presents a very general overview of a highly complex and changing legal area. So, if you are thinking about protecting your intellectual property then you will need to get your own professional legal advice.

2. Intellectual property rules and guidelines tend to refer to inventions and inventors rather than innovation and innovators, and this is a subtle but important distinction. Inventions are taken to refer to new scientific breakthroughs, ideas, and discoveries. Innovations can be thought of as the successful commercialisation of an

invention. Intellectual property protection can therefore facilitate the successful commercialisation of an invention, leading to innovation. But commercial success is not guaranteed, even if an invention passes the requirements for the granting of a patent.

3. The pharmaceutical industry is an interesting case. On the one hand governments want to encourage the extensive investment in the R&D required to develop new medicines, drugs and treatments. On the other hand governments want to limit the time that pharmaceutical companies can charge high prices in order to reduce their healthcare costs. For this reason the standard 20 year patent is reduced to 15 years in the pharmaceutical sector.

4. The licencing of intellectual property is one of the key elements of Chesbrough's Open Innovation model, as discussed in the previous section. In fact, Chesbrough contends that many large organisations only exploit a small fraction of their intellectual property, presenting opportunities to commercialise the so-called 'Rembrandts in the attic' through licencing.

5. Computer software is automatically protected by copyright. However, patenting software is a particularly grey area. It may be possible to patent software if it is integrated with hardware that delivers a new type of functionality. Clear? Then may I respectfully refer you to the excellent point made in Note 1.

QWERTY

Q: QWERTY

The word QWERTY[1] denotes the layout of a standard English language typewriter or keyboard, these being the first six keys on the top row from the left. So far so good, but what has this got to do with innovation? Well, the development of the typewriter and the adoption of QWERTY provides a good introduction to two important areas of innovation theory and practice; Standards and Dominant Designs.

The story of QWERTY begins in 1868 when the American inventor Christopher Latham Sholes was awarded a Patent for the typewriter. Unfortunately, it still required significant development to overcome several technical problems. Chief amongst them was the persistent jamming of the type bars. As an attempt to overcome this problem Sholes experimented with the arrangement of the keys to reduce the likelihood of adjacent keys being hit in quick succession, eventually settling on the QWERTY pattern. The QWERTY arrangement was not concerned with improving typing speed, and indeed actively slowing down typing speed may also have been an aim, as this also helped avoid jams.

Sholes eventually sold the rights to his patent in 1873 to the established small arms manufacturer E. Remington & Sons. They used their engineering capability to make further mechanical improvements, and then began production on a commercial scale. Gradually the typewriter with its QWERTY key arrangement became widely adopted, supported by the development of touch typing techniques that improved typing speed. Typewriter salesmen also liked the QWERTY arrangement because they could quickly punch out the word 'typewriter' to sceptical prospective clients using only keys from the top row (go on – try it!).

However, the fact remained that the QWERTY keyboard was not optimised for speed, and the mechanical jamming problem had long since been overcome. Surely then there would be a market for a keyboard optimised for typing speed that would soon make QWERTY obsolete? And that's exactly what American academic August Dvorak thought, patenting his Dvorak Simplified Keyboard (DSK) in 1936.

The DSK arrangement claimed greater typing speed and reduced typist fatigue, backed up by the results of US Navy trials.[2] However, despite these advantages the DSK failed to displace QWERTY, and after many years of fruitless effort Dvorak eventually died a bitter man. QWERTY had become the industry standard, and the market did not perceive that DSK offered sufficient improvements to become a new standard. For the English language, QWERTY remains the preferred standard keyboard layout to this day, even on Tablet devices with touch screen keys.

What does this story tell us? Well, for one thing it tells us that becoming an industry standard is highly advantageous because it can be very difficult for new entrants to displace your position. This is often due to high switching costs, for example the retraining required to adopt a new standard. A good example of this is the dominance of Microsoft's Windows operating system in the PC market. A large company wishing to switch to say Apple would need to write-off their investment in MS Windows, buy Apple's system, and retrain all their staff to use the new system (of course, switching to Apple requires Apple hardware as well as their operating system, an additional cost).

The chances of successfully developing an industry standard can potentially be enhanced by adopting a First Mover Advantage strategy, particularly if the intellectual property is protected through the use of patents, as in the case of QWERTY. However, rival standards are often developed simultaneously, leading to so-called 'Standard Wars' – battles for market dominance between incompatible technologies. Perhaps the most famous example of a Standard War was the rivalry in the Home Video market between Sony's Betamax system and JVC's VHS system.

Sony developed the Betamax video system in the 1970s, offering a licence to rival JVC. However, instead of accepting the licence deal JVC launched their own competing 'Video Home System', or VHS for short. VHS was characterised by reduced costs at the expense of slightly inferior picture and sound quality. Crucially, the two systems were incompatible – a Betamax video cassette could not be played on a VHS video recorder and vice-versa. Price conscious consumers started to side with VHS, and as their market share increased JVC enjoyed economies of scale, their costs (and prices) fell further, and the writing was on the wall for Sony.[3]

Sony did not make the same mistake twice. When DVD technology replaced video, Sony bet the farm on their 'Blu-Ray' system becoming the standard over Toshiba's rival 'HD DVD' system. Sony achieved early economies of scale by incorporating Blu-Ray into their own PlayStation games console. Eventually Blu-Ray prevailed as film distributors such as Warner Bros lost patience with incurring the costs associated with supporting two formats and sided with Blu-Ray.[4] Moral of the story – if you choose to engage in a Standards War (or indeed any war) then make sure that you win.

The concepts of Standards and Dominant Designs are closely related, and indeed the two terms are often used interchangeably by managers, engineers and even some scholars. However, according to Professor Scott Gallagher there are some important differences that once appreciated enable us to gain a more detailed understanding of the complex dynamics associated with developing new technologies, products and markets.

As we have seen in the above examples, the central role of Standards is to provide compatibility between products and their interfaces. This interconnectivity is particularly important when considering product-to-human interfaces, such as the QWERTY keyboard, where Tacit Knowledge relating to the Standard quickly diffuses throughout the market. A Standard is usually specific to the firm that created it, and is established either before or in parallel with the product development process.

In contrast to Standards, a Dominant Design is the result of an industry wide evolution of a product or class of products that eventually incorporates a range of design features and attributes that the market comes to expect as 'standard' (so you can see where the terminology confusion creeps in). A Dominant Design represents the industry's convergence on an accepted product architecture that once established becomes relatively stable over an extended period of time.

A good example of a Dominant Design is the development of the automobile. In 1771 Frenchman Nicholas-Joseph Cugnot test drove the very first automobile, powered by a steam engine.[5] Perhaps surprisingly steam engines were still used right up until the 1900s, but by this time electric and petrol powered automobiles had also been developed by firms such as the Olds Motor Vehicle Company and the Daimler Motor Company. Eventually the petrol engine powered automobile became the accepted Dominant Design adopted by the industry's major players such as Ford and General Motors. The petrol (or diesel) powered automobile has remains a dominant design over 100 years later, its efficiency and reliability steadily improved by a century of innovation. It's only relatively recently that electric vehicles are gaining market share, mainly spurred through governmental requirements to reduce greenhouse gas emissions and improve air quality.

The concept of Dominant Designs can be attributed to the seminal work of Massachusetts Institute of Technology (MIT) Professor James Utterback and the late Harvard Professor Bill Abernathy. They proposed that the dynamics of innovation shift as products and technologies progress through three phases of development; the Fluid Phase, the Transition Phase, and the Specific Phase. Within each of these phases they considered changes to four key factors:

1. **Product Innovation**

   During the initial Fluid Phase there is a flurry of Radical[6] Product Innovation from multiple firms experimenting with the application of a new technology. However, over time the rate of product innovation decreases as customer requirements and expectations become clearer during the Transition Phase, and eventually a Dominant Design emerges in the Specific Phase. Further product innovation becomes Incremental in nature, making relatively small improvements to the established product architecture.

2. Process Innovation

The Fluid Phase is also characterised by a relatively low rate of Process Innovation as firms concentrate on developing a saleable product. Processes tend to be improvised and inefficient, relying on skilled labour and the use of general purpose machinery. However, as the product design evolves through the Transition Phase and the size of the potential market becomes clearer there is a concerted effort to increase the rate of Process Innovation in order to increase production rates and reduce unit cost. Investment in Process Innovation continues until eventually the returns on further investment in process innovation diminish as both product design and manufacturing processes enter the Specific Phase and become mature.

3. Organisational Change

Organisational requirements also change as the firm shifts from being informal, innovative and entrepreneurial to becoming much more hierarchical, rigid and formalised. These new characteristics are associated with the managerial systems required to grow the firm rapidly and meet high production targets efficiently. Often the firm's free thinking founders get frustrated and leave during this transition phase (hopefully on very attractive financial terms).

4. **Market and Competitive Environment**

When a new technology is developed the market is characterised by many new firms seeking to establish their product's superiority. Market share tends to vary rapidly between firms, and new entrants are attracted by the potential size of the market and the appeal of high profit margins. As customer feedback and requirements become clearer and a Dominant Design emerges the emphasis shifts to reducing price through efficient manufacturing operations. Products begin to become undifferentiated and commoditised, prices fall, and the number of firms in the market reduces due to industry consolidation.

Utterback and Abernathy's dynamic innovation model has strong parallels with the Life Cycle concept discussed earlier in this book. In both cases a central argument is that firm innovation characteristics need to match the requirements of a dynamic market. This presents significant organisational challenges, and firms need to adapt their strategies, capabilities and management systems in order to remain competitive. Only by recognising and responding to the dynamic nature of the market can firms fully benefit from the development of new technologies into Dominant Designs.

SUGGESTED READING:

- **Anderson, P. and Tushman, M.** (1990). Technological Discontinuities and Dominant Designs: A Cyclical Model of Technological Change, *Administrative Science Quarterly*, 35(4), pp. 604–633.

- **David, P.** (1985). Clio and the Economics of QWERTY, *Economic History*, 75, pp. 332–357.

- **Gallagher, S.** (2007). The Complementary Role of Dominant Designs and Industry Standards, *IEEE Transactions on Engineering Management*, 54(2), pp. 371–379.

- **Liebowitz, S. and Margolis, S.** (1990). The Fable of the Keys, *Journal of Law and Economics*, 33(1), pp. 1–26.
- **Shapiro, C. and Varian, H.R.** (1999). The Art of Standard Wars, *California Management Review*, 41(2), pp. 8–32.
- **Suarez, F.F.** (1999). Battles for Technological Dominance: An Integrative Framework, *Research Policy*, 33, pp. 271–286.
- **Utterback, J.M. and Abernathy, W.J.** (1975). A Dynamic Model of Process and Product Innovation, *Omega*, 3, pp. 639–656.
- **Utterback, J.M.** (1994). *Mastering the Dynamics of Innovation: How Companies Can Seize Opportunities in the Face of Technological Change*, Boston MA: Harvard Business School Press.
- **Utterback, J.M.** (1995). Dominant Designs and the Survival of Firms, *Strategic Management Journal*, 16(6), pp. 415–430.

NOTES:

1. For the avoidance of doubt QWERTY is actually a real word, recognised in the Oxford English Dictionary and scoring an impressive 21 points in Scrabble.

2. I don't think the US Navy trialled the DSK at sea under battle conditions! At the time there were no photocopiers or computer printers, so big government departments like the Navy employed legions of typists. Therefore even modest improvements in typing speed would lead to big cost savings, hence the interest in the DSK.

3. I can clearly remember growing up during the Video Standard War. My father had bought a Betamax system, no doubt impressed

with its superior picture and sound quality. All my friends had VHS systems, and I had to grimly watch as the number of Betamax videos that could be rented at the local Blockbuster slowly dwindled down to nothing. Finally we had to throw away the Betamax and buy our own VHS recorder, much to everyone else's amusement.

4. Having been traumatised as a child by the Video Standard War I was determined not to repeat the experience with DVDs – so I waited until the HD DVD system actually died before investing in Blu-Ray. Behavioural economists would no doubt classify this as a classic example of 'Regret Avoidance', a common cognitive bias that leads to suboptimum decision making.

5. Cugnot's first test drive of his steam powered automobile did not end well – he crashed straight into a wall. Presumably this experience then led Cugnot to invent brakes, seatbelts and car insurance.

6. The concepts of Radical and Incremental Innovation are explored in the very next section of the book. But have a cup of tea first.

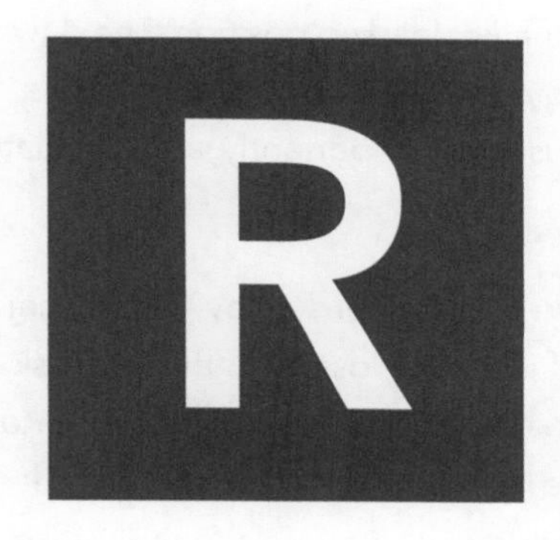

Risk and Radical Innovation

R: RISK AND RADICAL INNOVATION

A theme that has been developed throughout this book is that without Risk there is no innovation. However, most innovations are low risk in nature. These Incremental Innovations provide a series of small improvements in existing products, technologies, processes and services. Customers usually respond well to incremental innovation, and the investment required is relatively small. However, Incremental Innovations tend to be easy to copy and therefore yield no long-term competitive advantage. Greater payoffs can be achieved by investing in Radical Innovation,[1] which deliver much higher levels of improvement, are much more difficult for competitors to copy and can potentially deliver a sustained market leading position. The downside is that Radical Innovations are more expensive to develop, take longer to bring to market and perhaps most importantly are associated with inherently higher level of risk.

The concept of risk is characterised by the assigning of probabilities on the likelihood of incurring losses. In this way risk is distinct from the concept of Uncertainty, where it is not possible to generate reliable probabilities on the likelihood of various outcomes occurring. So for example, if you decide not to revise then you take a risk that you will fail your exam. You will calculate the probability of failing (say 50%), the consequences of failing (will you have the opportunity to re-sit, or will you get thrown-off your course?) and the benefits of not revising (spending the time on more high-value activities such as updating your Facebook status and playing Grand Theft Auto). However, you cannot calculate the probability of failing your exam because the bus taking you to the exam broke down causing you to miss it. This is uncertainty at work.

At the psychological level most people have a high degree of risk aversion, and because companies are made up of people organisational risk aversion is also widespread. Our understanding of risk aversion has been advanced recently by research in the field of Behavioural Economics.[2] This has led to the development of the concept of Prospect

Theory, which relates to the subconscious preference of avoiding losses rather than making gains.

This preference to avoid losses stems from our caveman ancestors, who for the most part were preoccupied with the tricky business of survival. If a caveman took a risk that resulted in increasing their provision of food, warmth or shelter then this would certainly be a positive outcome. However, if taking the risk resulted in a corresponding loss of food, warmth or shelter then this may well be fatal, hence the focus on avoiding losses. To demonstrate Prospect Theory at work in a more modern setting consider the following two-question exercise that I ask my students to undertake:

Question 1

You work for a company where your salary, bonus, and ongoing employment depend on your ability to make wise investment decisions for your employer. You are made aware of a one-off investment opportunity where you are offered the following options:

Option A: Make £1 million with no risk.

Option B: A 50/50 chance of either making £4 million or losing £1 million.

Which option do you choose, A or B?

Question 2

You work for a company where your salary, bonus, and ongoing employment depend on your ability to make wise investment decisions for your employer. You are made aware of an investment opportunity where you are offered the following options:

Option A: Make £10 million with no risk.

Option B: Ten individual investments, each with a 50/50 chance of either making £4 million or losing £1 million.

Which option do you choose, A or B?

Have you made your choices? This is what happens with my students:

For Question 1 the overwhelming majority choose Option A; making £1 million with no risk. They want to avoid the 50% probability of incurring the £1 million loss presented in Option B, even if there is a corresponding 50% probability of making a £4 million gain. The small minority who choose Option B tend to argue that they wouldn't mind a 50% chance of losing £1 million (and being fired) because a 50% chance to make £4 million seems quite attractive. I then take out a coin and give them a one-off 50/50 chance to be awarded either a distinction or a fail grade in my module. No-one takes up the offer!

For Question 2 the majority of students also select Option A, choosing to make £10 million with no risk rather than take the opportunity of potentially making £40 million with the risk of losing £10 million. But in this sequential investment situation it is the minority of students who selected Option B who get the opportunity to punch the air and cheer (yes, they really do) when they find out that they have made the correct choice. How so? We need to calculate the Expected Value of the ten investments as follows:

Expected Value = Number of Investments x Probability x (Outcome 1 + Outcome 2)

Expected Value = 10 x 0.5 x (£4 million – £1 million)

Expected Value = £15 million

So, the Expected Value of 'risky' Option B is £5 million more than the value of risk free Option A. The students who choose Option A have fallen victim to Prospect Theory; their desire to avoid losses has meant that they have miscalculated the relative gains.

Of course, the key to the attractiveness of Option B is that you get ten opportunities, and expect that five will succeed and five will fail.[3] The lesson for managing innovation is that you must expect some level of failure and should therefore not rely on pursuing a single 'all-or-nothing' innovation programme. A portfolio approach will help spread risk and mitigate individual programme failures. Ideally a portfolio will consist of both incremental and radical innovations, which brings us back to the issue of how to manage Radical Innovation effectively.

Professors Christopher McDermott and Gina O'Connor suggest that there are three broad strategic areas that firms must consider when managing Radical Innovation projects; choice of market scope, competency stretching, and the role of individuals.

1. Choice of Market Scope

When developing Radical Innovation programmes firms should start by considering the market scope. This will focus on either expanding an existing market or on creating a new market.

Existing Market: When expanding an existing market firms need to focus on:

- Ensuring that the Radical Innovation programme delivers a substantial benefit over existing market offerings.
- Ensuring that the threat of cannibalising[4] existing product lines is fully considered.

- Ensuring that any market resistance to the new technology is overcome.

Market Creation: When creating new markets firms need to focus on:

- Managing higher levels of inherent risk and uncertainty when compared to expanding an existing market.
- Accommodating the business unit creating a new market within the existing structure of the firm (or restructuring the firm).
- Ensuring that an effective business model is developed to fully take advantage of the potential offered by a market creating innovation.
- Convincing a sufficient number of customers to enter the new market. This point links into the previously discussed importance of Early Adopters.

2. Competency Stretching

Firms build up competencies over time that enable them to coordinate diverse production skills and integrate multiple streams of technology. However, for Radical Innovation programmes existing competencies need to be stretched, and this presents a significant organisational challenge. The risks associated with this can be managed in three ways:

Leveraging from Existing Competencies: Risk can be reduced by developing new competencies that are adjacent to the firm's existing competencies. For example, an aerospace firm with strong competencies in materials science could expand from steel to nickel, and then into titanium products. This is a lower risk route than having to develop brand new competencies in nonadjacent areas such as aerodynamic modelling or fluid dynamics.

External Partnerships: Alliances with external partners who already possess either technological or market competencies can reduce the risk, time and investment required to develop these internally. Partners need to be carefully selected and considerable attention given to the contractual framework governing areas such as Intellectual Property and the division of profits.

Effective Project Management: Competencies often develop organically over time. However, Project Management tools and techniques can be utilised to provide a much more structured framework for developing and managing competency development to support Radical Innovation.

3. The Role of Individuals

Ultimately the success of a Radical Innovation programme with be determined by the individuals within the firm. Three key issues emerge with respect to the role of individuals:

Leadership: There are two leadership roles that relate to Radical Innovation Development:

- Senior Sponsors are required to provide the financial backing and support for the programme, and if required to defend it from premature termination.

- Champions are required to provide the operational level enthusiasm and energy to overcome hurdles and keep the programme moving forward towards achieving its goals.

Teams: Radical Innovation programme teams require diversity in both breadth and depth of experience, including technical and marketing experience. Where the programme is a marked departure from the firm's current offerings then recruiting team members from outside of the firm can strengthen the team.

Networks: Experienced team members will have specific roles and functions. However, they will also have developed deep informal networks within and outside of the firm. These can provide access to information and knowledge that can be used to overcome problems and keep the programme on track.

The exact delineation between incremental and radical innovation will vary between firms, markets and industry sectors, and may in many cases be blurred and imprecise. However, categorising innovations as incremental or radical using a risk versus reward trade-off is an important discipline. It allows firms to effectively manage investment in their portfolio of innovations, and also identify the organisational factors that must be considered to support delivery of the overall innovation strategy.

SUGGESTED READING:

- **Genus, A. and Coles, A.** (2006). Firm Strategies for Risk Management in Innovation, *International Journal of Innovation Management*, 10(2), pp. 113–126.
- **Kahneman, D., Lovallo, D. and Sibony, O.** (2011). Before You Make That Big Decision…, *Harvard Business Review*, June, pp. 50–60.
- **Leifer, R., McDermott C., O'Connor, G., Peters, L., Rice, M., and Veryzer, R.** (2000). *Radical Innovation: How Mature Companies Can Outsmart Upstarts*, Boston MA: Harvard Business School Press.

- **McDermott, C. and O'Connor G.** (2002). Managing Radical Innovation: An Overview of Emergent Strategy Issues, *Journal of Product Innovation Management*, 19(1), pp. 424–438.

- **McLaughlin, P., Bessant, J., and Smart, P.** (2008). Developing an Organisational Culture to Facilitate Radical Innovation, *International Journal of Technology Management*, 44(3/4), pp. 298–322.

- **Slater, S.F., Mohr, J.J. and Sengupta, S.** (2014). Radical Product Innovation Capability: Literature Review, Synthesis, and Illustrative Research Propositions, *Journal of Product Innovation Management*, 31(3), pp. 552–566.

NOTES:

1. The terms 'Incremental Innovation' and 'Radical Innovation' have strong parallels with Clayton Christensen's terminology of 'Sustaining Innovation' and 'Disruptive Innovation', covered in Section D. According to Christensen, Sustaining Innovations are normally incremental in nature, but can also be more ambitious in scope (i.e. 'Radical'). Disruptive Innovations can be thought of as always 'Radical', but Radical Innovations are only 'Disruptive' if they (a) create a new market(s) and (b) disrupt an existing market(s).

2. Perhaps the most well-known behavioural economist is Nobel Prize winner Daniel Kahneman. If you wish to explore this area further I recommend his 2011 book *Thinking Fast, Thinking Slow*.

3. Some of you may be thinking, "But what if I am unlucky and win less than five times?" You are right to consider this possibility, especially if you have recently been crossed by a black cat or broken a mirror. You would no doubt turn to the field of binomial mathematics and calculate the probability of hitting a minimum number of wins and the corresponding Expected Value. But to save you the trouble, here is the full set:

Number of Wins	Minimum EV (£m)	Probability (%)
10 exactly	40	<0.1
9 or more	35	1.1
8 or more	30	5.5
7 or more	25	17.2
6 or more	20	37.7
5 or more	15	62.3
4 or more	10	82.8
3 or more	5	94.5
2 or more	0	98.9
1 or more	-5	99.9
0 exactly	-10	<0.1

So, you have an 82.8% probability of making back at least £10m, and only a 0.1% probability of making a loss. Not sure about you, but I'd take those odds any day.

4. Cannibalisation occurs when a company introduces a new innovative product (or service) to the market, but this has a negative impact on sales of the firm's established offerings. As an example, fear of cannibalisation was one of the principle factors behind the rejection of James Dyson's Dual Cyclone bag-less vacuum technology by incumbent vacuum cleaner manufacturers. The bag-less technology would have clearly hit their lucrative market in selling replacement bags.

   Similarly, when Apple introduced the iPhone they must have recognised that sales of iPods would be cannibalised (because the iPhone includes the functionality of an iPod). However, Apple took the view that it was better for them to cannibalise iPod sales than cede the smartphone market to rivals such as Samsung, Sony-Ericsson, and HTC. Ultimately, if you are not prepared to make your established products obsolete then your competitors will do it for you.

S-Curves

S: S-CURVES

In the section on Life Cycle it was shown that technologies eventually become obsolete and are replaced, as demonstrated by the demise of vinyl records, magnetic tapes, piston driven aero-engines, dot matrix printers, black and white TVs and dial-up internet. Given that this is the case, why is it that so many established companies seem to miss the opportunity to jump in time to catch the next wave of technological innovation, and instead yield market share to their rivals? This is a question that has perplexed corporate boardrooms and attracted significant academic attention. A key model that has emerged to map the progress and eventual replacement of technologies is the S-Curve.

Before diving straight into exploring the S-Curve it would perhaps be useful to define what exactly we mean by 'Technology'. As you might expect, there is no one unified definition of Technology because that would be too easy. However, Harvard Professor Clayton Christensen[1] provides a good starting point by defining Technology as:

> 'A process, technique or methodology embodied in a product design or in a manufacturing or service process which transforms inputs of labour, capital, information, material and energy into outputs of greater value'

In this way Christensen distinguishes Technology from Knowledge, where value is not necessarily unique to specific products or processes. Technology development is important because it enables companies to offer products or services with superior performance, lower cost, or both.

Right, back to S-Curves. The development of the S-Curve model is credited to former McKinsey consultant Robert Foster, who published his ideas in the 1986 book *Innovation: The Attackers Advantage*. As the title implies, Foster was a strong believer in First Mover Advantage, particularly when concerned with the introduction of new technology to the market. Like most good models the S-Curve is simple, powerful and easy to draw.[2] This is how it works:

The Y axis shows an appropriate measure of performance for the technology under consideration. For example, fuel economy is a useful measure of performance for aircraft gas turbine engines because it is valued by customers. Similarly, temperature capability is a good measure of the performance of turbine blades (because a higher temperature turbine gives a more fuel efficient engine). The X axis measures the R&D effort required to improve the performance of the technology. R&D effort is usually measured as either cumulative R&D spend, or time in years for industries with a steady rate of R&D expenditure.

When a new technology is first introduced additional R&D effort leads to fairly modest improvements in performance, represented by the gradually rising lower portion of the S-Curve. However, as the technology becomes better understood increases in R&D generate greater returns in performance, represented by the mid-portion of the S-Curve. This is the period of technology development where a high level of performance improvement is achieved for a given level of R&D effort.

However, at some stage the technology starts to mature and a point of inflection is reached where additional R&D investments generate reduced levels performance improvement, or what economists would call *'Diminishing Returns'*. Eventually no amount of additional R&D spend can improve performance as the natural limits of the technology are reached, shown by a flattening at the top of the S-Curve. At this point further performance gains can only be achieved by jumping to a new emerging technology that is in the early stages of its own S-Curve.

Of course, wise firms will not wait until their technology is obsolete before making the switch to the emerging technology. In this way the S-Curve can be used as a strategic tool to predict when the limits of a technology are likely to be reached, and when to make the switch. But unfortunately life is not quite so simple, and companies can fall into three major traps:

1. Premature Switching

This occurs when companies interpret the S-Curve data as showing that the technology is approaching maturity. They then switch to a new technology in order to generate further improvements in performance. However, technology development is not always predictable, and in the case of premature switching further significant performance gains could have been achieved by persevering with the original technology.

By switching prematurely the company has missed out on the opportunity to extend the life of the original technology and has instead taken on the risk and considerable expense of developing a new technology and incorporating this into their products and manufacturing operations. Furthermore, customers may need convincing that the new technology is worth adopting,[3] particularly as in the early stages it is unlikely to have superior performance to the original technology, and may in fact have reduced performance characteristics in some key areas, for example reliability.

2. Delayed Switching

The second trap arises when companies interpret the S-Curve data as showing that significant further improvements in performance are possible, but the reality is that technological obsolescence is fast approaching. In this situation they need to make a switch to an emerging technology that offers future performance levels beyond what can be achieved by persevering with the current technology. But their delay in making the switch allows competitors who have already made the switch the opportunity to achieve technological and performance leadership.

There are many reasons why companies fall into the Delayed Switching trap. There may be significant levels of Risk Aversion and N.I.H. Syndrome within the organisation. Power and politics may also play a strong role in persisting with a mature technology. For example, as mentioned earlier in the book, the Dutch company Philips was slow to spot the potential for compact disc technology. The reason? Many senior managers at Philips had built their reputations on the earlier development and commercialisation of magnetic tapes, and were therefore not keen to embrace a new technology.

The Delayed Switching trap is different from employing a Fast Follower strategy. Fast Followers are deliberately waiting for the emerging technology to become more mature, reliable, and attractive to customers before aggressively following the First Movers into the market with their own comparable (or often better) products.

3. Performance Myopia

The third trap is to focus on improving one particular performance characteristic at the component level and failing to appreciate that overall product performance may be highly dependent on additional factors, including the overall architecture of the product. As an example, let's return to the turbine blade in the aircraft gas turbine engine. There is no doubt that increasing the temperature capability of the turbine blade material will improve overall engine efficiency and hence fuel economy.

For this reason great improvements have been made in nickel superalloy materials technology, from refinements in alloy chemistry, to the development of unidirectional grain structures, and finally the emergence of single crystal blade technology. Each development is the result of extensive R&D, and has resulted in increased temperature capability.

> However, improved temperature capability can also be achieved by the development of a parallel technology, ceramic thermal barrier coatings. These allow the turbine blades to operate in environments well above the melting point of the nickel superalloy from which they are made.[4] A technology strategy based solely on the development of improved nickel superalloys would not have achieved such a result.
>
> Similarly, temperature capability is only one determinant of overall engine efficiency. Designers need to consider aerodynamic improvements, lightweight materials and novel engine architecture. So, for complex products a disproportionate focus on developing a single technology S-Curve is unlikely to deliver the optimum improvement in overall performance. To overcome this trap a more holistic approach to technology and performance management is required.

Having pointed out these traps you are probably questioning just how useful the S-Curve model is as a practical management tool. As a predictive model to precisely indicate when a technology will become obsolete and when firms should switch to a new technology it has its limits. But then again, can any tool deliver an accurate predictive capability? As Nobel physicist Niels Bohr once remarked: "Prediction is difficult – especially if it's about the future!"

Perhaps the value of the S-Curve model is that it forces us to think carefully about the way technologies develop, become obsolete, and get replaced, and how this needs to be incorporated into our corporate, product, and R&D strategies. Companies using S-Curves might not always get this right, but at least they are actively considering the strategic options available.

SUGGESTED READING:

- **Becker, R.H. and Speltz, L.M.** (1983). Putting the S-Curve Concept to Work, *Research Management*, 27(5), pp. 31–33.
- **Christensen, C.M.** (1992). Exploring the Limits of the Technology S-Curve. Part I: Component Technologies, *Production and Operations Management*, 1(4), pp. 334–357.
- **Christensen, C.M.** (1992). Exploring the Limits of the Technology S-Curve. Part II: Architectural Technologies, *Production and Operations Management*, 1(4), pp. 358–366.
- **Foster, R.** (1986). *Innovation: The Attackers Advantage*, New York: Summit Books.
- **Schilling, M.A. and Esmundo, M.** (2009). Technology S-Curves in Renewable Energy Alternatives: Analysis and Implications for Industry and Government, *Energy Policy*, 37, pp. 1767–1781.

NOTES:

1. Yes, this is the same Clayton Christensen whose work we discussed in the sections on Disruptive Innovation and Steve Jobs – so, fairly influential in innovation circles.
2. My attempt at a generic S-Curve example is shown below, demonstrating how the performance of Technology A develops as a function of R&D effort before further performance improvements are delivered by jumping to the development of Technology B.

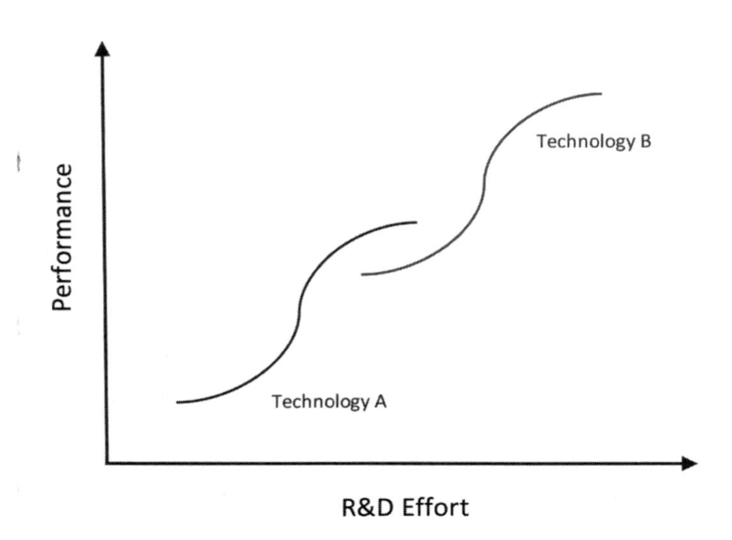

3. Adoption and the role of different customer types in technology diffusion is explored in more detail in the earlier sections on Early Adopters and Life Cycle.

4. Yes, this is true. Modern aero-engine high pressure turbine blades operate in an environment that is around 400°C (or 750°F) higher than the melting point of the base nickel superalloy, thanks to the use of thermal barrier coatings and a complex array of cooling air channels. Put another way, this is comparable to making a turbine blade out of ice and sticking it into a domestic oven set at maximum without it ever melting. I once told this to a pilot and he went a funny shade of white, but don't panic – it's perfectly safe!

Triple Helix

T: TRIPLE HELIX

Deoxyribonucleic acid (DNA) is the molecule that encodes the genetic instructions of living organisms. DNA has a complex intertwined double helix structure, first identified and isolated by Nobel Prize winners James Watson, Francis Crick and Maurice Wilkins. So far so interesting, but what is a Triple Helix, and what has it got to do with Innovation? The term Triple Helix was coined by Stanford Professor Henry Etzkowitz in the 1990s to help conceptualise the interaction between Universities, Industry and Government that drives innovation and economic development.

Governments tend to like economic development, particularly if it can be shown that they are actually contributing to it. There has therefore been no shortage of taxpayers money (sorry, *research funding*) to explore the Triple Helix paradigm. This research is used to inform policy decisions aimed at forging closer links between universities and industry, although why government intervention is necessary for this to happen is an interesting debate, implying that some form of *market failure* must be at work (as our friends the economists would say).

Universities tend to like to research their own contribution to innovation driven economic development, particularly if it attracts a large amount of government funding. There has therefore been a significant focus on developing the understanding of the Triple Helix in recent years, especially in the European Union and United States of America, with the emergence of books, journal publications, specialist conferences and even the founding of the Triple Helix Association (www.triplehelixassociation.org).

Industry is increasingly interested in using universities to complement – and in some cases substitute – the expensive business of conducting in-house R&D. In particular, using universities to conduct early stage speculative 'blue sky' research is highly cost effective, especially if this research is supported by government research grants and performed by knowledgeable and hardworking academics in well-equipped facilities.

This also aligns well with the development of the Open Innovation model, as discussed earlier in this book.

Overall, Industry is looking to gain access to new technology and knowledge to deliver a competitive advantage in the market, and this contributes to the overall economic development that governments seek to promote. So, at the risk of introducing another metaphor, the Triple Helix can be viewed as a virtuous circle between universities, government and industry, a win-win-win, if you like.

According to Etzkowitz there are four dimensions to the development of the Triple Helix:

1. The separate change and development of each of the three helices, for example through lateral ties amongst companies via strategic alliances or the adoption of an economic development mission by universities.

2. The influence and interaction of one helix on another, for example the role of government in setting overall economic policy influences both industry and universities.

3. The creation of new trilateral networks of universities, industry and government, for example by the creation of regional economic Clusters.

4. The effect of the Triple Helix on society over time, for example on how the meaning and position of science is being developed.

At the heart of the Triple Helix paradigm is the emergence of the so-called Entrepreneurial University. Traditionally universities had but two primary functions; to expand human knowledge via curiosity driven research and to teach students. Universities were funded by the state, but remained as largely autonomous institutions. Over the last 20 or so years several converging factors have changed this model.

Firstly, the demand for university education has dramatically increased, so that in the UK for example around 50% of young people go to university, compared with fewer than 10% in the recent past. This expansion has been driven by the emergence of the post-industrial Knowledge Economy, with policy makers convinced that only nations with a strong graduate workforce will be able to compete in the future.

The emergence of China as a low-cost manufacturing centre, and of India as a low-cost service and IT outsourcing centre has reinforced this view in western economies. And the Chinese and Indians don't want to be low-cost providers forever – they are rapidly expanding their own knowledge-driven capabilities and graduate workforce. So global competition in the knowledge economy is going to increase as developing nations move up the value chain.

Secondly, the money required to finance this expansion of university education has unexpectedly run out following the 2008 global banking crash, restricting government funding for universities.

Thirdly, governments have increasingly viewed universities as instruments to drive a wide range of policy initiatives. For example, in the UK universities are now expected to:

- Develop graduate employability skills such as team working, problem solving and communication skills as well as develop the more traditional academic competencies such as critical thinking and scientific enquiry.

- Provide a much stronger focus on teaching quality and student satisfaction, measured by increases in student 'contact hours', and by increasing the percentage of students who are awarded top degrees.

- Promote diversity, equality, inclusion, and social mobility, for example by reducing entrance requirements for disadvantaged students that have been failed by the state education system.
- Focus their research primarily on national industrial and business priorities rather than curiosity driven research i.e. only research with a clearly defined economic benefit is deemed worthwhile.
- Commercialise their research and Intellectual Property through developing profit-making spin-out companies and science parks (thus supplementing the ever reducing government funding).
- Be the catalysts and focal points for local economic regeneration and employment.

For Entrepreneurial Universities economic development has become a core mission. The Entrepreneurial University has moved from a generator of new knowledge to a generator *and* commercialiser of new knowledge. In this way Entrepreneurial Universities embrace the spirit of commercial organisations whose interest in knowledge has always been closely tied to economic utility.

To a large extent the change required to transform a traditional university into an Entrepreneurial University is dependent on the collective attitudes and core beliefs of faculty members. For some, the naked dash for research commercialisation is a betrayal of the ideals that underpin the purpose of a University and an attack on academic freedom.

For others, commercialising research is a natural extension of a university's mission, opening up opportunities to the benefit of the institution, the individual researcher, the wider economy and society. For example, if the entrepreneurial spirit of a university research team led to the discovery, rapid development and commercialisation of a new treatment for cancer then the economic and societal benefits would be substantial.

Etzkowitz himself remains an energetic and charismatic focal point for the Triple Helix. Recently I had the opportunity of watching him deliver a keynote speech at a conference in Amsterdam,[1] complete with blazer and straw hat (that's how I like my professors), in which he convincingly made the case for the shifting mission of universities in directly driving innovation and economic development. Overall, the Triple Helix is an elegant and memorable term to describe University – Industry – Government interactions and to frame the research investigating this area.

SUGGESTED READING:

- **Etzkowitz, H. and Leydesdorff, L.** (1997). *Universities and the Global Knowledge Economy: A Triple Helix of University-Industry-Government Relations*, London: Cassell Academic.

- **Etzkowitz, H. and Leydesdorff, L.** (2000). The Dynamics of Innovation: From National Systems and 'Mode 2' to a Triple Helix of University-Industry-Government Relations, *Research Policy*, 29(2), pp. 109–123.

- **Etzkowitz, H.** (2011). Triple Helix Circulation: The Heart of Innovation and Development, *International Journal of Technology Management and Sustainable Development*, 7(2), pp. 101-115.

- **Leydesdorff, L., Etzkowitz, H.** (1996). Emergence of a Triple Helix of University–Industry–Government Relations, *Science and Public Policy,* 23, pp. 279–286.

- **Leydesdorff, L., Etzkowitz, H.** (1998). The Triple Helix as a Model for Innovation Studies, *Science and Public Policy* 25(3), pp. 195–203.

- **Leydesdorff, L.** (2000). The Triple Helix: An Evolutionary Model of Innovations, *Research Policy*, 29(2), pp. 243-256.

NOTES:

1. And in case you were wondering the answer is no, the fact that this conference was held in Amsterdam had no bearing at all on my decision to attend, not even a tiny bit…

User-Centred Innovation

U: USER-CENTRED INNOVATION

As mentioned earlier in the book, Henry Ford famously proclaimed that if he had asked his customers what they wanted then they would have said "a faster horse". His point was that customers often lack the insights and imagination to predict their future requirements, and therefore innovation is best left to the experts. However, what if Ford's customers had turned around and said, "A low cost, reliable automobile powered by an efficient internal combustion engine" and then started providing Ford with their own drawings of what this would look like? And what if Ford's customers continued to make their own customised modifications to his Model T (for example, painting it a different colour than black)? This alternative scenario is the basis of User-Centred Innovation, a key model developed by Massachusetts Institute of Technology (MIT) professor Eric von Hippel.[1]

Von Hippel captured his thinking on User-Centred Innovation in his 2005 book *Democratizing Innovation* (which you may be interested to know is free to download and well worth a read). By 'democratization' von Hippel simply means that the users of both products and services are able to innovate for themselves, and are no longer reliant on being dictated to by firms pursuing traditional 'Manufacturing-Centred Innovation'.

The advantage of User-Centred Innovation is that users get exactly what they want by utilising their knowledge of how a product or service works in practice to customise and optimise performance. Furthermore, users are in a unique position to develop customised solutions through in-field experimentation and trial-and-error type methodologies. Von Hippel cites examples such as open source software development, sports equipment and surgical equipment as areas where users have developed their own innovative products for their own use.

So who exactly are these 'users'? Von Hippel proposes that users are either firms or individuals that expect to benefit from using a product or service. This is in contrast to 'manufacturers' who expect to profit from selling a product or service. It is therefore argued that because it is users who directly benefit from the utility of innovations they are in a unique position to optimise benefits, costs and functionality.

However, not all users are the same. Von Hippel characterises 'Lead Users' as being at the leading edge of the market and significantly ahead of the majority of users. These Lead Users will be at the forefront of innovation and will expect to gain high benefits from developing solutions to their needs. There is therefore a high degree of overlap with the Diffusion literature and the concept of Early Adopters, discussed earlier in this book.

Lead Users need to consider several factors before making an Innovate-or-Buy decision. These include:

- Is there an existing product in the marketplace that meets their needs?
- Do they have the time and funding to develop their own solution?
- Will the benefits of a custom solution outweigh the costs (and risks) of development?

Von Hippel argues that there is a growing trend for users developing their own customised solutions. This is driven by:

- Increased user heterogeneity and diversity, therefore only a small number of users want exactly the same mass produced product.
- An associated willingness by users to pay for the development of a customised solution.
- Increased computer power enabling users to access information, communicate and collaborate, and design their own increasingly complex products.

- The emergence of low-cost manufacturing subcontractors, particularly in China, who can manufacture users' unique designs.

- The growth of user communities who can share experiences and best practice, for example surgeons, mountain bikers and surfers.

Von Hippel also suggests that the actual act of innovating may also be intrinsically rewarding for users, as well as help infuse an innovative culture throughout user firms. He also notes that users tend to share information and knowhow without seeking to protect their Intellectual Property, so-called 'free revealing'. This helps to reinforce the strength of user communities as well as increase the rate of innovation diffusion. This is particularly valuable where the innovation has a societal benefit, for example medical and surgical tools and techniques, or educational services.

Does this mean that the days of traditional manufacturers are numbered? Von Hippel conceptualises a system where in many sectors 'User-Centred Innovation' and 'Manufacturing-Centred Innovation' co-exist and are mutually reinforcing. Often manufacturers can produce low cost high volume product platforms which then undergo customisation from users. And manufacturers themselves can cultivate a network of Lead Users to help inform their new product development strategy.

Von Hippel notes a body of research that points to a new product launch success rate of around 27%; or put another way, over 70% of new product launches fail. Clearly this is inefficient and exposes manufacturers to high levels of commercial risk. Ironically, it may very well be this high failure rate that drives manufacturers to launch non-customised products, leading to subsequent User-Centred Innovation.

However, developments in technology have also led to higher levels of customisation. For example, car manufacturers offer a wide range of user options relating to engine type, transmission, wheels and trim.

Smartphone users customise their experience through their selection of apps (and apps themselves are often developed by users).

Perhaps the most potentially significant technological innovation in recent years is the development of 3D printers. As the name suggests, these printers allow users to produce three dimensional plastic, resin, or even metallic shapes of their own unique designs. This technology may firmly put the means of production in the hands of users, and eventually every home may be transformed into an innovation factory. Or alternatively the main application may be to allow established manufacturers to rapidly develop their own customised products.[2]

Only time will tell, but what is clear is that users will continue to have an important role to play in the design and development of innovative products and services.

SUGGESTED READING:

- **Bogers, M., Afuah A., and Bastian B.** (2010). Users as innovators: A review, critique and future research directions. *Journal of Management*, 36(4), pp. 857–75.

- **Rothwell, R. and Gardiner, P.** (1985). Invention, Innovation, Re-Invention and the Role of the User, *Technovation*, 3, pp. 167–186.

- **von Hippel, E.** (1978). Users as Innovators, *Technology Review*, 80(3), pp. 30–34.

- **von Hippel, E.** (1986). Lead Users: A Source of Novel Product Concepts, *Management Science*, 32(7), pp. 791–805.

- **von Hippel, E.** (1988). *The Sources of Innovation*, New York: Oxford University Press.

- **von Hippel, E.** (2005). *Democratizing Innovation*, Cambridge MA: MIT Press.

- **Urban, G. and von Hippel, E.** (1988). Lead User Analyses for the Development of New Industrial Products, *Management Science*, 34(5), pp. 569–582.

NOTES:

1. Yes, this is the same Eric von Hippel that we came across in the sections of Disruptive Innovation and Open Innovation, so he really is quite influential.

2. A good source for information and discussion on 3D printers is *Economist* magazine, for example their February 2011 article 'The Printed World: Three-Dimensional Printing from Digital Designs will Transform Manufacturing and Allow More People to Start Making Things'.

Venturing

V: VENTURING

For large organisations innovation is seen as an engine driving growth through the development of new products, services, processes and business models. However, the internal barriers to innovation are many, for example organisational boundaries, risk aversion, and Not-Invented-Here Syndrome. It seems that somewhere along the line the entrepreneurial spirit that originally made the business successful has been lost. In an effort to overcome these barriers many established businesses turn to Venturing[1] to reignite entrepreneurism and kickstart growth.

Venturing is nothing new. For example, according to Professor Henry Chesbrough[2] in the 1960s and 1970s around 25% of the Fortune 500 companies ran venturing programmes. Well-known companies that have introduced venturing programmes include Adobe, Intel, Lucent, Exxon, Nokia, Cable & Wireless, Unilever, Procter & Gamble, British Telecom, Siemens, 3M and Xerox.[3] Venturing generally takes one of three forms:

1. **Internal Corporate Venturing (ICV)**

   ICV is when the company creates a new business that operates from within the company's organisational domain, often with a high degree of alignment with existing capabilities.

2. **External Corporate Venturing (ECV)**

   ECV is when a company creates a new business that operates outside of the company's organisational domain, so-called 'Spin-offs' or 'Spin-outs'. The parent will either wholly own or retain a significant equity stake in the new business.

3. **Corporate Venture Capital (CVC)**

   CVC is when a company invests in a start-up or early phase company that has originated from outside of the organisation. It therefore acts in a similar manner to a Private Venture Capital (or Private Equity) company, but with the potential benefit of a longer time horizon, potentially larger funding available, and the support of the parent company's resources and capabilities.

While companies will want to see a healthy financial return on their investment, venturing often has a strong strategic element. For example, venturing can:

- Infuse the company with an entrepreneurial dynamic that promotes further innovation and growth across the core business.
- Enable the company to experiment with and pilot disruptive technologies that may support the core business, become the future core of the business or provide opportunities to move into adjacent markets.
- Develop complementary businesses that create demand for the company's core products and services. For example Intel invested in businesses that drove demand for its microprocessors.
- Reinforce an Open Innovation strategy where the company is already looking for access to external opportunities and ideas, and investing directly in these opportunities is a natural extension.
- Enable the company to attract, motivate and retain talented employees. This is particularly important for technical specialists who may be tempted to leave and form their own Private Equity backed start-up.[4]
- Provide commercialisation opportunities for technologies developed by R&D that do not fit the company's core business, thereby increasing the return on R&D investment.

- Drive overall company strategy, or in some cases venturing actually *is* the company strategy (for example Richard Branson's Virgin Group).

Turning the archetypal slow, lumbering and bureaucratic corporate behemoth into a fast, nimble, and entrepreneurial business creating machine by the mere waving of the Chief Executive's magic wand is quite difficult to achieve, as witnessed by the extensive graveyard of failed venturing programmes. For example, Lucent Technologies' New Ventures Group was set up to commercialise technology developed from the Bell Laboratory. However, following the telecom downturn Lucent sold 80% of its interests in the New Ventures Group to the British private capital management company Coller Capital in 2002.

This is one of the examples given by Professors Robert Burgelman and Liisa Välikangas, who suggest that the enthusiasm for Internal Corporate Venturing (ICV) tends to be cyclic in nature, depending on the financial resources available for venturing and the prospects of the core business to deliver the performance demanded by investors. They propose a cycle consisting of four potential situations:

1. ICV 'Orphans'

This describes a situation where there is sufficient uncommitted financial resource to support ICV activity, but the prospects of the core business are relatively strong. Therefore there is little motivation for senior management to consider ICV. In this environment some entrepreneurial activity will occur on an ad-hoc basis, but these 'Orphan' projects then drift along without any central coordination or support.

2. 'All-Out Drive' for ICV

This describes a situation where again there are sufficient uncommitted financial resources to support ICV, but this time the prospects of the core business are much weaker. Senior management are therefore very likely to launch an 'All-Out Drive' for ICV activity, usually by creating a new venture group or division to centrally manage this activity. Any existing 'Orphan' projects will be incorporated into this new structure.

3. ICV 'Irrelevance'

Now, while the prospects of the core business look good there are no uncommitted resources to launch ICV activity. Therefore ICV becomes an 'Irrelevance' to the company and management focus is directed to exploiting the core.

4. 'Desperately Seeking' ICV

This is the worst of both worlds, where the core business is weak but there is a lack of uncommitted financial resource to support ICV activity. Any ICV projects launched are likely to be highly uncertain, under-resourced, and have a high risk of failure. Desperation indeed.

Venturing programmes can fail for a number of reasons. For example, the overall macroeconomic cycle will often determine the availability of financial resource and the strength of the core business. Senior management may be impatient and have unrealistic expectations of the time taken for a venturing programme to succeed (particularly if they are already 'desperate'). Conversely, a successful venturing programme may also face internal resistance, particularly if it makes the performance of the core business look poor by comparison, or if it starts to exert unwelcome strategic influence.

V: VENTURING

So what can be done to improve the chances of successful venturing? Research from the likes of Robert Burgelman, Rita Gunther McGrath and Jeffrey Covin points to several common themes:

1. **Build Leadership Capability**

   Leaders should view venturing as an integrated and continuous component of the strategy making process. This means that all senior executives should share a commitment for venturing.

2. **Establish Realistic Expectations**

   Venturing is a long-term commitment, not a short-term exercise to shore-up the company's finances. Ventures therefore need to be protected from unrealistic expectations. Similarly, measuring the performance of ventures with the same metrics used for measuring the established core business should be avoided.

3. **Manage with a Portfolio Mindset**

   Companies should focus on developing a portfolio of venturing projects that spread risk and allow for the failure or cancellation of individual projects. It is the performance of the overall portfolio that should be the primary concern of senior management.

4. **Capture Knowledge and Learning**

   Successful venturing programmes deliver more than simply financial returns. The knowledge and learning generated from ventures are key outputs, and must be captured and incorporated into the core business.

Overall venturing can make an important contribution to a company's financial position, strategy development and knowledge base. Venturing provides an effective mechanism to escape the constraints of the core business and explore new opportunities that will sustain innovation, entrepreneurism and growth. Companies should therefore adopt a long-term strategic approach to managing venturing.

SUGGESTED READING:

- **Burgelman, R.A. and Välikangas, L.** (2005). Managing Internal Corporate Venturing Cycles, *MIT Sloan Management Review*, 46(4), pp. 26–34.
- **Chesbrough, H.** (2000). Designing Corporate Ventures in the Shadow of Private Venture Capital, *California Management Review*, 42(3), pp. 31–49.
- **Chesbrough, H.** (2002). Making Sense of Corporate Venture Capital, *Harvard Business Review*, 80(3), pp. 90–99.
- **Covin, J.G. and Miles, M.P.** (2007). Strategic Use of Corporate Venturing, *Entrepreneurship Theory and Practice*, 31(2), pp. 183–207.
- **McGrath, R., Keil, T. and Tukiainen, T.** (2006). Extracting Value from Corporate Venturing, *MIT Sloan Management Review*, 48(1), pp. 50–56.
- **Napp, J.J. and Minshall, T.** (2011). Corporate Venture Capital Investments for Enhancing Innovation: Challenges and Solutions, *Research Technology Management*, March-April, pp. 27–36.

NOTES:

1. This section talks about 'Venturing', but many theorists and practitioners use the term 'Corporate Venturing'. So don't get confused – they are taken to describe the same phenomenon.

2. Chesbrough extensively researched the venturing activities of American high-tech companies before hitting academic gold with his Open Innovation theory (see section 'O').

3. Xerox is a particularly good case of a company that has launched several venturing programmes, with mixed success. More on Xerox later in the book under 'X'.

4. Typically the reward package for a senior research scientist working for a large company is a comfortable salary, pension, and perhaps some stock options. Or alternatively they can leave, found their own start-up with private equity backing, and end up owning 10% of a $250m company after five years. At least that's the Silicon Valley dream. But by offering venturing as an option to commercialise research the scientist can directly benefit financially via an equity stake in the new venture (if it is successful) without taking on the risk of going it alone. The parent company also benefits from the growing new venture, and also holds on to the scientist.

Waves

W: WAVES

The concept of Waves incorporates the fields of Economics and Entrepreneurship, therefore presenting a good opportunity for innovation students, scholars and practitioners to explore these important areas. We start by discussing the work of Russian economist Nikolai Kondratiev and his development of the Long Wave Cycle to map economic fluctuations and technological change. We then move on to discuss the Austrian economist Joseph Schumpeter's work on Entrepreneurship, and in particular his notion of Creative Destruction.

Kondratiev[1] was the founder and director of Moscow's prestigious 'Institute of Conjecture'. Building on the work of earlier (but not so well-known) economists Kondratiev proposed that economic activity followed long wave cycles of prosperity, recession, depression and then recovery, before a new wave begins with prosperity again (hooray). Each economic cycle spans 50 years and can be mapped against waves of significant technological change. Wave 1 coincides with the Industrial Revolution, and an extension of this theory can take us into the 21st Century.

Wave 1	1780-1830	Cotton, Iron, Water Power
Wave 2	1830-1880	Steam Power, Railways, Steamships
Wave 3	1880-1930	Electricity, Chemicals, Steel
Wave 4	1930-1980	Cars, Electronics, Oil, Aerospace
Wave 5	1980-2030	Computers, Telecoms, Internet

So, the observant amongst you will note that we are living through Wave 5, but what comes next? Economists have proposed that Wave 6 may include the development of areas such as nanotechnology, hydrogen based energy and robotics. Others suggest that Kondratiev's long wave cycle theory, while fairly elegant, doesn't really work all that well in practice. For example, Daniel Smihula suggests that rather than a series of equally spaced 50 year cycles each new wave has a reduced duration i.e. the cycle is continuously shortening and therefore Wave 6 may have already started. Ultimately technological change may become so rapid that waves will become indistinguishable from each other.

A notable economist who was influenced by Kondratiev's work on long wave cycles was Joseph Schumpeter. Schumpeter held a professorship at the University of Bonn, before emigrating to the United States before the onset of the Second World War to join Harvard University. He believed that it was shifts in technological innovation that caused economic cycles, disputing the established theory favoured by classical economists of stable economic equilibrium[2] achieved by price competition.

Schumpeter proposed two models to demonstrate how innovation drives economic cycles, his Mark I Model and then later a (less influential but still valid) Mark II Model:

Mark I Model

Schumpeter's Mark I Model proposes that new firms emerge using innovation to disrupt markets and threaten the position of existing firms. These new firms are founded by entrepreneurs and compete not on price, but by creating one of five sources of significant change:

- Introducing new products, or making an improvement to an existing product.
- Creating new markets, particularly export markets in new territories.
- Securing new sources of raw materials or semi-manufactured goods.
- Developing new methods of production that have not yet been validated.

- Creating new types of industrial organisation, particularly if the new organisation leads to the formation of a monopoly.

Schumpeter's view of an entrepreneur is someone who has the ability, vision and determination to bring about these significant changes and threaten the viability of incumbent firms.[3] In this respect entrepreneurs are different to business owners and salaried managers who undertake 'routine' work. Crucially, entrepreneurs use innovation to create change and disrupt markets.

Building on earlier work by Kondratiev (and also Karl Marx) Schumpeter envisioned what he describes as a cycle of 'Creative Destruction', where the creation of new entrepreneurial firms causes the destruction of established firms that can no longer compete. This cycle of creative destruction[4] drives economic growth, although as more firms enter the market there will be a gradual erosion of profitability until the next wave of innovation occurs.

Mark II Model

And then he completely changed his mind! Schumpeter developed his Mark II Model while a professor at Harvard, arguing that it is in fact the large incumbent organisations that have the capabilities and resources required to drive innovation and economic growth, with small start-ups unlikely to be able to compete. In this model the entrepreneur is not someone who starts their own business, but rather an employee or manager of a large organisation that behaves in an entrepreneurial way, i.e. by utilising innovation to drive change.

So which model is correct? I would suggest that they are in fact complementary. There are many examples of the Mark I model at work. For example Apple, Microsoft, Google, Dell, Starbucks, Walmart, Facebook and Ryanair are all firms 'created' by entrepreneurs that grew rapidly to disrupt existing markets. On the 'destruction' side of the equation large corporate failures include Nortel, Kodak, Texaco, Kmart, Royal Bank of Scotland and MG Rover Group.

And yet there are many large organisations that have survived (and have in fact prospered) for decades, for example General Electric, Boeing, Ford, Procter & Gamble, DuPont and Exxon Mobil. What separates successful organisations from the failures is the ability to retain their entrepreneurial spirit and innovate. Effective Innovation Management is therefore a key capability for firms, although as we have seen in previous sections this is never easy to achieve.

SUGGESTED READING:

- **Abernathy, W.J. and Clark, K.B.** (1985). Innovation: Mapping the Winds of Creative Destruction, *Research Policy*, 14(1), pp. 3–22.
- **Drucker, P.** (1985). *Innovation and Entrepreneurship*, New York: Harper and Row.
- **Kondratiev, N.** (1935). The Long Waves in Economic Life, *Review of Economic Statistics*, 17, pp. 6-105.
- **Korotayev, A., Zinkina, J. and Bogevolnov, J.** (2011). Kondratieff Waves in Global Invention Activity, *Technological Forecasting and Social Change*, 78(7), pp. 1280-1284.
- **Schumpeter, J.A.** (1934). *The Theory of Economic Development: An Inquiry into Profits, Capital, Credit, Interest, and the Business Cycle,* New Brunswick: Transaction Books.
- **Schumpeter, J.A.** (1939). *Business Cycles: A Theoretical, Historical, and Statistical Analysis of the Capitalist Process*, New York: McGraw-Hill.

- **Schumpeter, J.A.** (1942). *Capitalism, Socialism, and Democracy*, New York: Harper.

- **Smihula, D.** (2010). Waves of Technological Innovations and the end of the Industrial Revolution, *Journal of Economics and International Finance*, 2(4), pp. 58-67.

- **Spencer, A., Kirchhoff, B. and White, C.** (2008). Entrepreneurship, Innovation, and Wealth Distribution: The Essence of Creative Destruction, *International Small Business Journal*, 26(1), pp. 9-26.

NOTES:

1. Kondratiev can also (somewhat confusingly) be written as Kondratieff, and his Long Wave Cycle theory is often simply referred to as K-Waves.

2. Other economists, for example Israel Kirzner, argue that there is not an absence of equilibrium, but rather a temporary disequilibrium that entrepreneurs spot and exploit. Therefore Kirzner proposes that the notion of economic equilibrium still holds when considering new venture creation and entrepreneurship.

3. So Schumpeter's entrepreneur is very much a person who possesses a set of distinctive personality traits. The 'Born or Made' / 'Nature versus Nurture' argument is a large area of academic enquiry with significant policy implications. If entrepreneurs are born then policy should be directed at identifying entrepreneurs. If entrepreneurs can be made then policy should be directed at encouraging and supporting people to become entrepreneurs. This area is beyond the scope of this book, but to summarise 85 years of research in five words – 'Anyone can become an entrepreneur'!

4. Creative destruction is sometimes referred to as 'waves of creative destruction', the 'winds of creative destruction' or 'Schumpeter's gale' ('Schumpeter's wind' not sounding quite right somehow).

Xerox

X: XEROX

As I write this X-rated section Halloween has just passed, complete with trick-or-treaters dressed as ghosts, skeletons, vampires and zombies. In the world of Innovation Management (and indeed Corporate Strategy) there is a particularly chilling story told in hushed tones to board rooms, directors and executives. It is the story of how a once powerful and successful corporation wasted opportunity after opportunity to profit from innovation, despite investing billions of dollars in R&D. This corporation then found its market share eroded by nimble Japanese competitors, while simultaneously having to watch new companies such as Apple and Microsoft rise to dominate brand new technology markets. The name of this company is (whisper it…) Xerox, and it seems that no Business School programme is complete without getting the students to pick over the bones of Xerox's extensive catalogue of failures, while a wise professor sadly shakes their head.[1] What insights from Xerox can be drawn that can help us manage innovation? Let's find out…

Xerox is a major US corporation operating in the photocopying, printing and document management markets. Founded in 1906 as the Haloid Photographic Company it changed its name to Xerox in 1961 following its development of the world's first commercial photocopying machine, the snappily named '914'. Today Xerox employs some 140,000 staff, and regularly posts revenues of $20bn and operating profits of $1bn. That's not bad going, and I think that Xerox's management deserve more than a little credit.

However, critics (and investors) would point out that performance is relative, and Xerox's profits are dwarfed by Microsoft and Apple. They would also point out that while Microsoft and Apple founded their businesses on the back of the Personal Computer it was Xerox that actually invented, and then ignored, the PC – a fairly significant oversight, and hence all the talk about 'fumbling the future'.

In fact, the PC is one of a long line of innovations developed by Xerox but successfully commercialised by other players in the market. The source of Xerox's innovations is their Palo Alto Research Centre, or PARC for short. Nestling in the hills overlooking Silicon Valley, PARC was developed in the 1970s by Chief Executive Peter McColough. His vision was to establish a world class R&D centre that would allow Xerox to become a dominant force in the new information age. PARC recruited the world's leading scientists who pioneered major breakthroughs.

However, it soon became clear that only the technology directly supporting Xerox's core photocopying business was being adopted, the rest being rejected by senior management at Xerox's Connecticut headquarters as too risky/unproven/expensive. This proved extremely frustrating for PARC's scientists, many of whom left to join other organisations, or started up their own businesses.[2] Three examples that illustrate the problems associated with PARC are the development of the Xerox Alto, the Ethernet and finally the Laser Printer.

1. Xerox Alto

Many consider the Xerox Alto as the first true personal computer. Developed in 1973 it was ahead of its time, featuring a cathode ray tube screen, a mouse type control device, QWERTY keyboard and 'windows'-type operating system allowing users to open programmes and files by clicking onscreen icons. However, Xerox could not see its commercial potential, and its use was restricted to PARC itself and a few government contracts.

All this changed in 1979 when a certain Steve Jobs persuaded Xerox to give him a private tour of PARC by reportedly offering Xerox the opportunity to purchase 100,000 heavily discounted Apple shares. Apple went on to become the world's most valuable company, so this would seem to be not a bad deal for Xerox. Once inside Jobs was immediately stunned by the Xerox Alto, and could not believe that Xerox had not seen its enormous commercial potential.

Before you could say "Insanely Great!" Jobs had instructed his own team to replicate the Xerox Alto,[3] and quickly marketed his own Apple Lisa machine followed by the all-conquering Macintosh series. Meanwhile, Microsoft cleaned up on PC operating systems. Belatedly Xerox entered the market with their Xerox Star series of workstations, but by this time cheaper rivals were also entering the market and Xerox were eventually forced to accept defeat.

2. Ethernet

One of the pioneering features of the Xerox Alto was the development of the world's first working Ethernet to link up machines, including an early version of email. This was quite handy, because it allowed PARC scientists to exchange data and communicate with each other efficiently. But what about the commercial potential?

Ethernet connectivity soon became embedded in Xerox products, allowing a variety of equipment configurations to be joined with a single cable. However, Xerox could not see any applications beyond this, and was happy to grant the inventor of Ethernet, Robert Metcalfe, a license to exploit the technology for a token one-off fee of $1,000.[4] Big mistake.

Metcalfe had by this time already left Xerox, and teamed up with Digital Equipment Corporation (DEC) and chip giant Intel to develop a standard based around his Ethernet protocol. And as we discovered in the section on QWERTY, developing a standard has tremendous commercial significance. Metcalf quickly secured venture capital funding and launched his own company, 3Com, to take Ethernet technology to the mass market.

3Com eventually went public in 1984, at one point surpassing the value of Xerox itself, before eventually being bought by HP for $2.7bn in 2009. Or put another way, if Xerox themselves had successfully commercialised Ethernet technology then they would have more than doubled their market value.

3. Laser Printer

One of the problems with both the Xerox Alto and Ethernet technology was that they were seen as outside of Xerox's core product portfolio. But what about printing? Surely copying and printing were strategically aligned? Certainly that's what PARC scientist Gary Starkweather thought when he conceived the world's first laser printer. This could even be incorporated into a Xerox photocopier, giving users the ability to both copy and print documents directly from a computer.

But there was incredible resistance from Xerox management. "There is no future in computer printing." "Lasers are too expensive and unreliable." "Surely if there is a market then IBM would be doing it." And so on. However, one of the characteristics of PARC was that it was relatively straightforward to work on personal pet projects, and so undeterred Starkweather designed and built his laser printer anyway, first unveiling it in 1969.

And once Xerox's management saw what it was capable of they were... afraid. Afraid that on-demand high quality printing would render their copiers obsolete. And so the laser printer was mothballed – until IBM launched their own laser printer in 1976. This prompted Xerox to finally launch their own competing '9700' model the following year. Laser printing has eventually gone on to become a multibillion dollar business for Xerox, vindicating Starkweather (who by this time had left in frustration to join... Apple).

So what is going on? Well, if you have read this book from the start you may already have some insights. Many organisations struggle with Ambidexterity – managing the current needs of the business with an exploitation mindset (copiers) while simultaneously focusing on developing future opportunities with an exploration mindset (PCs, Ethernet, laser printers). Not-Invented-Here Syndrome also seems to be at work within Xerox itself. PARC was based in Silicon Valley on the west coast of the United States, whereas the headquarters of Xerox was based on the east coast in Connecticut.

It is not just these 3,000 or so miles separating PARC with the HQ. PARC scientists were often perceived as disconnected, aloof, and more interested in technology itself than commercialisation; inventors rather than innovators. Meanwhile senior management at HQ were commercially experienced at selling photocopiers, but lacked the entrepreneurial flair required to spot new market opportunities. As Schumpeter might say, both entrepreneurship *and* innovation are required for economic growth

And yet Xerox has resisted Schumpeter's *creative destruction* and are still going; so the question shifts from 'What if?' to 'What now?'. Harvard professors Scott Anthony and Clayton Christensen[5] suggest in their excellently titled 2012 paper 'The Empire Strikes Back' that developing disruptive services under the leadership of CEO Ursula Burns is paying dividends for Xerox. Facilitated by the 2009 acquisition of Affiliated Computer Services for $6.4 billion, services are expected to account for two-thirds of Xerox's future revenues. So it appears that business model innovation will play as much a part in Xerox's future as product innovation and technology development have in the past.

SUGGESTED READING:

- **Anthony, S. and Christensen, C.** (2012). The Empires Strike Back: How Xerox and Other Large Corporations are Harnessing the Force of Disruptive Innovation, *Technology Review*, 115(1), pp. 66–68.

X: XEROX

- **Chesbrough, H.** (2002). Graceful Exits and Missed Opportunities: Xerox's Management of its Technology Spin-Off Organisations, *Business History Review*, 76(4), pp. 803–837.
- **Gladwell, M.** (2011). Creation Myth: Xerox PARC, Apple, and the Truth about Innovation, *The New Yorker*, 87(13), pp. 44–53.
- **Hitzik, M.** (2000). *Dealers of Lightning: Xerox PARC and the Dawn of the Computer Age*, New York: Harper Business.
- **Loutfy, R. and Belkhir, L.** (2001). Managing Innovation at Xerox, *Research Technology Management*, 44(4), pp. 15–25.
- **Smith, D.K, and Alexander, R.C.** (1988). *Fumbling the future: How Xerox Invented, and then Ignored, the First Personal Computer*, New York: Morrow.

NOTES:

1. When considering cases like Xerox it is important that we are mindful of Phil Rosenzweig's Halo Effect concept that we came across (ironically) in the section on Steve Jobs. It's easy to look back in hindsight and judge the effectiveness of management decisions. It's a lot more difficult to make those decisions at the time.

2. Of course, being based in Silicon Valley meant that there were many employment opportunities for PARC scientists, as well as plenty of Venture Capital money available to back start-ups. In September 1993 *Fortune* magazine published a lead article somewhat harshly titled 'The Lab that Ran Away from Xerox'! This is the double-edged sword associated with locating your research within a Cluster. You can attract talented people, but they can leave just as easily.

3. Steve Jobs was particularly impressed with the mouse device. Noting that the Xerox mouse cost $300 and was prone to breaking

down, Jobs instructed his team to design a mouse with three characteristics; to cost less than $15 to manufacture, to last for two years, and to be usable on a standard office desk surface "and my Levi's jeans!"

4. Just to confirm, this is not a misprint. Xerox really did ask Robert Metcalf for just $1,000 for a licence to develop Ethernet technology, which he used to found a business eventually sold to HP for $2.7 billion.

5. Yes, this is the same Clayton Christensen that we came across in the sections on Disruptive Innovation, Steve Jobs, Radical Innovation, and S-Curves. So, fairly influential in the world of Innovation Management!

Yellowtail

Y: YELLOWTAIL

The original title of this book was going to be *The A to Z of Innovation Management (but not including the letter Y)*. I felt that this would be slightly humorous, and make up for the fact that there was a distinct shortage of Innovation Management concepts beginning with Y. However, as the book progressed, and possibly after a glass or two of wine, it struck me that there was an excellent opportunity to include the case of Yellowtail to illustrate one of the latest concepts in Innovation (and Strategic) Management; Blue Ocean Strategy.

Blue Ocean Strategy (BOS) is the brilliantly memorable name given by INSEAD Business School Professors W. Chan Kim and Renée Mauborgne to their 2005 book, along with the enticing subtitle 'How to create uncontested market space and make the competition irrelevant'. Well let me tell you, if you are an executive under pressure to hit your quarterly numbers then uncontested market space and irrelevant competition sounds ideal. Furthermore, after studying 108 business launches the authors made the following claims:

- Only 14% of these business launches utilised BOS, the remaining 86% simply competed in existing markets.
- However, these 14% BOS business launches accounted for 38% of all Revenues.
- In addition, these 14% BOS business launches accounted for 61% of all Profits.

Or in other words, the business launches that utilised BOS were more profitable by a factor of almost ten! Strong claims, and perhaps these contributed to Kim and Mauborgne's book notching up sales of 3.5 million and counting.[1]

According to Kim and Mauborgne the foundation of BOS lies in the concept of Value Innovation. Traditional businesses focus on head-to-head competition in existing markets, resulting in price competition and shrinking profits – a bloody Red Ocean full of sharks. In contrast, Value Innovation switches the focus from competing in existing market space to creating new market space that represents a leap in value for both customers and vendor. Value Innovation aims to deliver enhanced utility for customers together with lower prices, breaking the traditional trade-off between functionality (or quality) and price.

So, this sounds attractive but not very straightforward to achieve. Creating new markets requires creativity, and staring at a blank sheet of paper for hours on end waiting for inspiration to strike is unlikely to be successful (as we have seen in the section on Ideation). Fortunately, Kim and Mauborgne propose a simple framework to help businesses create a new competition free market, the tranquil Blue Ocean full of supernormal profits.

The framework starts with acquiring a detailed understanding of an existing sector or market. If you are already competing within this existing sector or market then you should already have this to hand.[2] Then just apply the following four steps:

Reduce: Which factors should be reduced well below the industry standard?

Raise: Which factors should be raised well above the industry standard?

Eliminate: Which of the factors that the industry takes for granted should be eliminated?

Create: Which factors should be created that the industry has never offered?

Once this four-step process has been applied then you should end up with a new value proposition that opens up a Blue Ocean. Kim and

Mauborgne give several examples of how this has been applied in practice including Yellowtail, a wine created by the Australian company Casella Wines to crack the US market.

At $20 billion per annum the US wine market is the third largest in the world. However, the US is only 31st in the world for per capita wine consumption. Now many strategists would conclude that Americans simply prefer drinking beer and spirits, and focus their resources on competing in these markets. However, Casella Wines interpreted the data as showing that there was significant latent demand for wine in the US that could lead to the creation of a Blue Ocean.

The existing US wine market was characterised by several factors. These included vineyard prestige, complexity and depth of flavour, wine ageing, specialist terminology and wine show awards and medals. In addition, the market was polarised by premium versus budget price points, with sales supported by brand development and advertising through television and print media.

However, many Americans perceived this system as intimidating and pretentious, finding it difficult to choose what to buy, and not enjoying the complex taste that the winemakers were striving for. In short, the process of buying and enjoying wine was a real barrier, and unsurprisingly they opted for the easier option of choosing beer or spirits. Casella Wines therefore decided to create a wine that challenged the industry's business model and assumptions, launching Yellowtail in July 2001.

Yellowtail aimed at establishing itself as a fun and easy to enjoy wine, with a simple flavour, only two varieties (one Shiraz and one Chardonnay), and strongly emphasising its Australian origin. This was achieved by the not-very-subtle approach of adopting a kangaroo logo and the tagline 'The essence of a great land… Australia'. They also hired 'ambassadors' to staff wine retailers dressed up in typical Australian outback clothing (shorts, oilskin jacket, bushman's hat) to recommend the wine.

Suddenly choosing what to buy was easy, fun and adventurous, and at an attractive price point of US$6.99 a bottle, set below prestige wines but above budget wines. By analysing Casella's strategy using a Blue Ocean framework we get the following:

Reduce: Wine Complexity, Wine Range, Vineyard Prestige, and Price versus Prestige Wines.

Raise: Price versus Budget Wines, Retail Store Experience and Display Clarity.

Eliminate: Specialist Terminology, Ageing, and Traditional Marketing Channels.

Create: A New Easy Drinking Category, Ease of Selection, and a Sense of Fun and Adventure – Buying more than just wine.

Did this Blue Ocean Strategy work? You bet it did! While the established vineyards were horrified at this new pretender, Yellowtail became the fastest growing brand in the history of both the US and Australian wine industries. It quickly outstripped sales of both French and Italian wine imports, and by 2003 was the number one red wine in the US, beating even home produced Californian wines. By 2004 Casella was shipping over 11 million cases of Yellowtail to the US and struggling to keep up with demand – a nice problem to have.

The Blue Ocean framework can be applied to many successful businesses that have created new markets. Take for example the Irish budget airline Ryanair which started in 1985 with one Boeing 737 and quickly grew to become the largest airline in Europe, exceeding the market capitalisation traditional carriers such as British Airways. Comparing Ryanair to the established airline market we can see how the BOS framework distinguished their offer and created a new market for budget air travel:

Reduce:	Ticket prices, ticket flexibility, baggage allowance, crew wages, legroom and customer service.[3]
Raise:	Aircraft turnaround speed, punctuality, and number of seats per aircraft.
Eliminate:	In-flight meals, in-flight entertainment, seat choice, business class, main hub airports, intercontinental flights and travel agents.
Create:	Regional airport network, internet booking channel, self-check-in and new demand for short city breaks.

However, before we get too carried away it is important to note that there are several criticisms of Blue Ocean Strategy. Firstly, what do you do to stop competitors entering your nice new Blue Ocean and turning it a nasty shade of blood red. Kim and Mauborgne suggest that this can be avoided by keeping prices low to deter market entrance and by striving to continuously develop the Blue Ocean to further distance it from the competition.

It can also be seen from the Yellowtail and Ryanair examples that it can be difficult for established players to enter a Blue Ocean while constrained by their existing business model. For example, prestige vineyards would find it hard to launch a lower priced, non-complex, easy drinking wine while preserving their core brand. Similarly, traditional airlines such as British Airways have found it difficult to reduce their structural overheads sufficiently to offer a budget service.

A second criticism is that the research methodology used by Kim and Mauborgne has some weaknesses. For example, they examine the performance of Blue Ocean companies without adequate use of a non-Blue Ocean control group. Also, the authors have applied Blue Ocean frameworks retrospectively to explain the success of companies like Casella Wines. But these companies did not actively sit down and systematically reduce/raise/eliminate/create to create new markets, their strategy just evolved that way. The line of causality between BOS and enhanced performance has therefore not yet been established.

A third criticism is the charge that Blue Ocean Strategy is merely a clever way of reframing existing strategic models. These include Lieberman and Montgomery's concept of First Mover Advantage and Porter's notion of achieving competitive advantage via a Differentiation strategy. The originality and utility of Blue Ocean Strategy as a new strategic framework is therefore not fully accepted, particularly within academia. Even some of the terminology can appear indistinct. For example, how exactly is the term Value Innovation distinct from the term Blue Ocean Strategy, or are they one of the same thing?

However, while criticisms of Blue Ocean Strategy may be valid I would suggest that it still serves as a thought provoking and useful concept for practitioners aiming to take an innovative approach to market and business model development. You may not be able to avoid the Red Ocean of competition indefinitely, but your Blue Ocean should be highly profitable while it lasts.

SUGGESTED READING:

- **Buisson, B. and Silberzahn, P.** (2010). Blue Ocean or Fast-Second Innovation? A Four-Breakthrough Model to Explain Successful Market Domination, *International Journal of Innovation Management*, 14(3), pp. 359–378.

- **Kim, W. and Mauborgne, R.** (2004). Blue Ocean Strategy, *Harvard Business Review*, 82(10), pp. 76–84.

- **Kim, W. and Mauborgne, R.** (2005). Blue Ocean Strategy: From Theory to Practice, *California Management Review*, 47(3), pp. 105–121.

- **Kim, W. and Mauborgne, R.** (2005). Value Innovation: A Leap into the Blue Ocean, *Journal of Business Strategy*, 26(4), pp. 22-28.

- **Kim, W. and Mauborgne, R.** (2005). *Blue Ocean Strategy: How to Create Uncontested Market Space and Make the Competition Irrelevant.* Boston MA: Harvard Business School Press.

NOTES:

1. As you may recall from section D, this is about 3,495,000 more copies than most business books sell.

2. However, if you don't yet have a detailed understanding of the market or sector in which you are competing then perhaps you may wish to take the opportunity to develop this at your earliest convenience...

3. A 2007 *Economist* article asserted that Ryanair had become "a byword for appalling customer service", with a "cavalier attitude to passengers" and a "deserved reputation for nastiness". Ouch!

   I've searched for a suitable (and printable) defence from Ryanair's famously abrasive CEO Michael O'Leary. Here it is:

   "Why are we carrying 81 million passengers if we're this terrible? We have the lowest fares, we have brand-new aircraft and we have the most on-time flights."

   So there!

Z

Zipf's Law

Z: ZIPF'S LAW

One of the themes of this book is the role of technology in disrupting existing markets, and perhaps no recent technology has had quite the effect as the internet. Firms such as Google, Amazon, Apple, Facebook, Netflix, Alibaba and eBay have risen by fully harnessing the opportunities offered by the internet, connecting consumers and reducing transaction costs. Meanwhile, established industries such as retail, film, music and book publishing have all felt the full force of Schumpeter's gale of creative destruction.

In particular, the fact that consumers can easily access an almost limitless supply of digital content has led to the emergence of the so-called 'Long Tail' of demand that shifts digital age economics away from simply catering for the narrow preferences of the mass market. The principle that helps underpin the Long Tail business model is **Zipf's Law**, the title of this final section of our Innovation Management journey.

Believe it or not, before the advent of the internet age business was a lot simpler. If for example you were a record company, then you would aim to sign artists that had the potential to sell a large amount of records (and later, CDs). Why? Because even large record retailers like Tower and HMV only have a limited amount of shelf space, and they don't want to have this taken up with stock that doesn't shift. It's the same story with books, films, or in fact any good or service that relies on access to finite space in order for it to be bought or consumed.

And this model worked very nicely for many years, supported by Italian mathematician Vilfredo Pareto's 80/20 rule.[1] This is the observation that in many areas just 20% of inputs leads to 80% of outputs. So 20% of a firm's products lead to 80% of sales revenues, 20% of our effort leads to 80% of our productivity, 20% of students take up 80% of my time. You get the picture. For the music industry it therefore follows that 20% of artists (U2, The Rolling Stones, Pink Floyd, Madonna, Queen, Jay Z, Adele, etc.) generate 80% of revenues, and so there is not much point in nurturing upcoming talent that doesn't have the potential to go platinum (at the very least).

A phenomena related to the Pareto Rule was observed by Harvard linguist George Zipf in his 1949 study of word-use frequency.[2] Zipf discovered that the second most used word is used half as often as the first, the third most used word is used a third as often as the first, the fourth most used word is used a quarter as often as the first, and so-on in an entirely predictable pattern.

This relationship is now known as Zipf's Law, and has been observed to hold for a number of other areas such as demographic distributions and notably city population sizes within countries (the second biggest city is half the size of the first, the third biggest city is one third of the size of the first, and so on).[3]

Zipf's Law follows what is called a Power Law Distribution, producing a curve in the form of 1/x that starts high but then slowly decreases, approaching (but never quite reaching) zero – the *Long Tail*. Traditional business models that rely on finite retail space and serve geographically constrained consumers focus firmly on the upper part of the curve that represents the most popular goods, services, music, books and films because this is the most efficient use of the space available.

But while this may make economic sense, there is a hidden cost. Focusing solely on the upper part of the curve leads firms to try and replicate past successes, therefore adopting a very risk averse and incremental approach to innovation. For example, witness the succession of dull Hollywood films that stick to well-worn formulas, or the seemingly endless production line of 'boy bands' and other bland imitations. Creativity, diversity and consumer choice are therefore stifled under the relentless pressure of coming up with the next mega-hit.

However, the internet has enabled an alternative business model to evolve where firms don't have to rely on hits, and can instead make high returns by serving multiple specialist niches in the almost infinite Long Tail portion of the power curve. This model was popularised by the writer Chris Anderson in an article for *Wired* magazine, which led to his 2006 book entitled *The Long Tail.*

According to Anderson, firms such as Google, Amazon and Apple not only profit from the Long Tail, but make *more* profit from the Long Tail than with traditional hits or bestsellers. The power of the Long Tail arises from the combination of the following five factors:

1. **Distribution:**

   Content is either digital in nature, requiring no physical retail space (think iTunes or eBooks), or else can be stored in warehouses that are considerably cheaper to operate than high street retail space (think Amazon). There are therefore no longer physical barriers such as limited retail shelf space preventing distribution of products or services from the Long Tail portion of the power curve.

2. **Costs:**

   Costs are significantly reduced, particularly for digital content. For example, a traditional CD may retail at $15, but an iTunes track download is $0.99. Low prices also help drive demand. According to Anderson halving music download prices from $0.99 to $0.49 triples sales, increasing revenues by 50%. In addition, alternative music subscription models such as Spotify have the effect of reducing costs per track even lower, for example $9.99 per month for unlimited access to music. Low costs also act as a disincentive for consumers to seek free 'pirate' music downloads.

3: Search:

Consumers can now easily search and find exactly what they are looking for online, however obscure or 'niche', and this actually fuels demand for specialist products. For example, I might like 'Hit' band Metallica and be able to buy their latest CD from a high street retailer such as HMV, but now I can easily access specialised content from their early (and much better) days as well as explore other less well known Californian Thrash bands like Exodus and Testament.

4. Scale:

Because consumers can now easily find exactly what they are looking for, even specialist niche markets have global scale, making them economically attractive. For example, if the local HMV in my home town stocks Exodus and Testament CDs, there is likely to be very low demand. OK, just me then. But through online aggregators such as iTunes this niche market now encompasses the whole of the UK, Europe, North America and the world, potentially leading to thousands of sales.

5. Exploration:

Consumers are also introduced to *new* content by internet aggregators and are therefore encouraged to further explore a niche or an adjacent niche. For example Amazon makes new recommendations based on your previous searches and purchase history and these recommendations have independent reviews and ratings from other members of your 'Tribe'. Similarly, YouTube recommends new content based on search terms, and within a few clicks you can find yourself in new spaces aligned with your interests.

Anderson clearly sees the development of niches within the Long Tail as the future of the entertainment-based industries. However he also points out other areas where the Long Tail is at work. For example Google's pay-per-click advertising model makes most of its revenues from a global Long Tail of small businesses rather than Fortune 500 giants.

The brewer Anheuser-Busch has increased its beer range from 26 in 1997 to 80 in 2007, and now includes organic beer, microbrews, craft beer, beer for women, beer for Texans and even gluten free beer available to order online. Anderson goes on to give more examples, including online education, boutique fashion, low cost travel, artisanal foods, comics, sports, video streaming and specialist radio.

Does this mean that the world of the 'Hit' is now dead? Not quite. Anderson segments Hits into three broad categories:

Type 1: Authentic Top-Down Hits that are excellent and appeal to a large audience, for example the film *Avatar*, the band Pink Floyd or Formula 1 racing.

Type 2: Synthetic Top-Down Hits that are inherently poor products that rely on over-marketing to get people to try them. I'm sure you can think of many examples...

Type 3: Bottom-Up Hits that emerge through word of mouth and grassroots support. Examples include the rise of the band Nirvana, mixed martial arts such as the Ultimate Fighting Championship (UFC) or the *Girl with the Dragon Tattoo* series of books.

Anderson argues that Type 1 Hits will continue to do well on merit, and that Type 3 Hits will become more frequent as the internet facilitates the spread of recommendations via word-of-mouth. However, firms still engaged in pushing poor Type 2 Hits onto an unsuspecting public are likely to find their margins squeezed as negative internet fuelled word-of-mouth takes hold and consumers realise that there is now much more choice readily available.

In this respect the Long Tail model may therefore act as the catalyst for higher levels of creativity and innovation in the future, and I think that this is an appropriately optimistic thought to end on.

SUGGESTED READING:

- **Anderson, C.** (2006). *The Long Tail: Why the Future of Business is Selling Less of More,* New York: Hyperion.
- **Brynjolfsson, E., Hu, Y.J. and Smith, M.** (2006). From Niches to Riches: Anatomy of the Long Tail, *MIT Sloan Management Review,* 47(4), pp. 67–71.
- **Brynjolfsson, E., Hu, Y.J. and Simester, D.** (2011). Goodbye Pareto Principle, Hello Long Tail: The Effect of Search Costs on the Concentration of Product Sales, *Management Science,* 57(8), pp. 1373–1386.
- **Fleming, L.** (2007). Breakthroughs and the Long Tail of Innovation, *MIT Sloan Management Review*, 49(1), pp. 69–74.
- **Zipf, G.** (1949). *Human Behaviour and the Principle of Least Effort,* Cambridge MA: Addison Wesley.

NOTES:

1. Pareto's 80/20 rule does have its limitations and critics. Firstly, the 80 and 20 are percentages of different things (typically revenues and number of products or profits and number of products). They therefore don't have to add up to 100, and may actually be 80/15,

80/10 or any other combination. In addition, it is not clear which of these variables to select or hold constant. For example, are revenues or profits the right variable? Finally, the 80/20 rule can cause a fixation with identifying and stocking only the top 20% of products, when:

a) You won't know what the top 20% is without trialling a wide range of products.

b) You need to be continuously refreshing the top 20% as technology changes and consumer preferences evolve.

c) The Long Tail argues that in internet enabled markets the majority of revenues and profits are in multiple specialist niches outside of the top 20%.

2. 1949 was obviously a kinder and gentler time for academics to explore areas of research with no obvious direct commercial significance.

3. See for example Gabaix, X. (1999). Zipf's 'Law for Cities: An Explanation', *Quarterly Journal of Economics*, 114(3), pp. 739-767.

Pulling It All Together: Five Emerging Themes

So, at the end of the book you now know more about these 26 key Innovation Management topics than 99% of the population. But can these individual topics build into broader themes to help develop how we conceptualise and implement Innovation Management? In my view there are five themes that begin to emerge:

1. Innovation and Idea Generation

The starting point for innovation is idea generation, and this is an area that has received significant attention in the literature. I suggest that we have explored seven topics which relate to this. Adopting a disciplined process of Ideation to identify new opportunities is likely to be more successful that simply waiting for inspiration to strike. Ideas can originate from within the organisation, for example through internal R&D centres such as Xerox's PARC laboratory. A robust Knowledge Management system to facilitate information sharing can also act as the catalyst for idea generation.

However, external sources of ideas are also important. For example, ideas can be generated via external networks and the adoption of Open Innovation. User-Centred Innovation and collaboration with Universities via a Triple Helix model can also facilitate idea generation. Finally, the location of the organisation in Clusters of similar organisations and research intensive universities can support idea generation via the attraction and development of creative and entrepreneurial individuals and firms within a concentrated area.

2. Innovation and Strategic Management

Commercial success starts with a strong strategy, and a strong strategy incorporates innovation. Strategies which neglect to consider innovation are inherently weak, because they fail to place sufficient emphasis on developing new profit streams for the medium to longer term. This in turn leaves the organisation vulnerable to more innovative competitors who can better meet the future needs of customers. The strategic management of innovation should therefore be one of the top priorities of directors, executives and senior management.

Within the A to Z of Innovation Management I suggest that there are 11 topics that are strongly related to the strategic management of innovation. The concept of Horizons allows managers to explicitly plan for supporting short, medium and longer term projects to underpin growth. Risk and Radical Innovation forces organisations to consider the right balance of risk and reward, and the mitigation of risk through developing a portfolio of innovation projects. First Mover Advantage is a key strategic consideration concerning market entry timing.

Product Life Cycle and the identification of Early Adopters to support market growth are also strategic factors to be considered. QWERTY introduces us to the important areas of Standards and Dominant Designs. The strategic management of Intellectual Property, for example via Patents also requires focus. The adoption of Open Innovation to develop external networks and accelerate innovation has been a successful strategic shift for many organisations. Finally, the concepts explored in the sections on Venturing, Yellowtail, and Zipf's Law direct us to consider the important area of designing effective and innovative business models.

3. Innovation and Organisational Factors

However, simply having a strategy that incorporates innovation is not sufficient for success. There are a range of organisational factors which significantly influence innovation, and I suggest that this book has identified ten topics which impact this area. Boundaries determine the internal configuration of the organisation. However, these can become barriers to innovation, particularly if they restrict the development of effective information sharing and Knowledge Management. The organisational interface with external agents is also an important consideration, for example through the adoption of Open Innovation, or via external Venturing.

Establishing organisational structures and behaviours which support the development of an Ambidextrous organisation ensures that exploitation of the core business does not limit the exploration of new opportunities. Not-Invented-Here Syndrome and Risk aversion are two interrelated phenomena that affect individual and collective behaviours and inhibit innovation. Leadership and the role of the individual within an organisation is an important consideration, as we have seen through the section on Apple CEO Steve Jobs. The concept of Management Innovation challenges organisations to develop new ways of working.

Finally, the study of organisations such as Xerox can generate significant insights into the organisational dynamics of innovation, although we must exercise a degree of caution in how we interpret such cases – what works for one company might not work for another, and vice-versa. We also have to recognise that real management decisions must be made without the benefit of hindsight.

4. Innovation and Technology Management

Innovation driven by the development of new technology is a key area of practitioner and academic interest, and there are ten topics that relate to this. Clayton Christensen's concept of Disruptive Innovation explores how technology development can create new markets and disrupt existing markets. Kondratiev's Long Wave Cycle theory helps us chart the rise and fall of technology, and its impact on economic growth.

S-Curves help us conceptualise how the performance of a new technology can be developed and improved over time, and when to 'jump' to a new technology as obsolescence approaches. The S-Curve model has strong parallels with the Life Cycle concept, where a new technology establishes a niche market before crossing the *chasm* into the mass market. However, growth eventually plateaus and then declines as a superior technology emerges. The establishment of a new technology and jump into the mass market is highly dependent on the support of Early Adopters, who are prepared to take on higher levels of Risk associated with a new technology.

The section on QWERTY explores the role of technology in the development of Standards and Dominant Designs. New technology results in the generation of intellectual property, which firms may protect through Patents in order to prevent rivals from copying. However, new technology *per se*, even if it can be patented, does not guarantee a commercial success. Much of the new Technology developed by Xerox's PARC laboratory was never successfully commercialised. It took the entrepreneurial mindset of someone like Steve Jobs to see the commercial potential of technology such as the personal computer and wireless mouse.

5. Innovation and Economic Policy

The final theme is the linkage between innovation and economic policy, and this book has covered 6 topics related to this. Kondratiev's Long Wave Cycle theory charts the relationship between technology development and economic cycles. This was extended by Joseph Schumpeter, who identified the role of the entrepreneur in economic growth, utilising innovation to disrupt existing markets via a process of *Creative Destruction*. The role of entrepreneurship on jobs creation was explored by David Birch, who identified the key role of high growth Gazelle firms.

Government support for innovation takes several forms. Legislation relating to Patents is designed to encourage innovation and investment in research and technology development, although the advent of patent trolls and sharks has recently called into question the effectiveness of the patent system. The support of a Knowledge Economy via the expansion of the graduate workforce is another area of government intervention. The research outputs of universities are also a source of innovation, leading to the so-called Triple Helix of University – Industry – Government interaction. Universities are also key players in the establishment of Clusters, where governments attempt to replicate the success of Silicon Valley in various industry sectors, with varying degrees of success.

Final Thoughts

As you can see, some topics such as Open Innovation, Venturing and Early Adopters span several themes. Similarly, some firms may argue that topics such as Knowledge Management should be seen as strategic in nature, because for them it impacts competitiveness. Whenever we try to simplify and order complexity there will always be a degree of subjectivity involved!

The 26 topics covered in this book are not intended to provide a precise roadmap of what you need to do to enhance innovation within your own organisations. They are intended to provide an overview of the key concepts, theories, models and frameworks that underpin our understanding of Innovation Management. My hope is that armed with these you will feel better equipped to embark on your own innovation journey.

Acknowledgements

In a rare moment of modesty Sir Isaac Newton stated that "If I have seen further than others, it is by standing on the shoulders of giants". Well, I'm not standing on the shoulders of giants. I'm on the ground looking up, just trying to make sense of what is going on in the expanding field of Innovation Management. So my first acknowledgement must go to the giants in the field, the likes of Schumpeter, Drucker, Rogers, Christensen, von Hippel, Chesbrough, Moore, Hamel, Utterback, and many others. My hope is that this book has helped to show the linkages between the different facets of Innovation Management and encouraged the reader to explore the field in greater depth.

There is a well-worn saying that "in theory, practice is the same as theory – but in practice it's not!" So my second acknowledgment goes to the managers and academics who have taught me where the balance lies. Neil Walker, Sarah Walker, Mike Cope, Sam Beale, Paul Spilling, Mike Hicks, Don Boulton, Andy Moore and Neil Glover have all helped me to develop my management thinking and experience. In academia Professors Simon Mosey, Andy Lockett, Graeme Currie, Deniz Ucbasaran, Steve Brammer, Nigel Driffield and Simon Collinson have all supported my (almost) swan-like transition into a scholar.

Aristotle once said that "teaching is the highest form of understanding". I now know what he meant! My third acknowledgement therefore goes to the 1,500 Innovation Management Undergraduate, Masters, and MBA students that I have had the opportunity to teach over the last few years. They have helped me to develop my understanding of Innovation Management, and have also provided useful feedback on draft PDF versions of this book. Some have even said that they might buy it (I have your names).

ACKNOWLEDGEMENTS

My final acknowledgement goes to my family and friends who have supported me through the process of writing this book, which if I'm honest slowed quite a lot at about the letter 'P'. So thanks to my parents Brian and Diane for enthusiastically reviewing an early draft, my brothers Andy and Pete for always being available for a beer, and to my wife Françoise and children Annabel and Estelle for the endless supply of tea and for encouraging me to finally get it published…

About The Author

Following a Degree and PhD in Engineering from the University of Birmingham, Dr Mike Kennard started his career with Rolls-Royce plc where he worked for over ten years in various technology management positions. These included Programme Manager for the company's global Research and Technology Programme and leading the development of the fan module for the Trent 1000 engine designed to power Boeing's 787 Dreamliner.

In 2006 Mike was awarded a scholarship to study for an MBA at Nottingham University Business School, where he graduated with distinction. After this Mike joined the University of Nottingham, first as a Business Development Executive and then as an Innovation Research Fellow, working with a global healthcare company to identify and overcome organisational factors that impact innovation and growth.

He then joined Aston Business School in 2010 as MBA Director, before returning to the University of Birmingham in 2013 as Programme Director for Business Partnerships and Senior Lecturer in Strategy and Innovation. Mike is also a Chartered Engineer, Member of the Institute of Engineering and Technology, and a Visiting Lecturer at Grenoble École de Management and the Singapore Institute of Management.

Mike's teaching, research and consulting focuses on strategic decision making, innovation driven growth strategies, and identifying and overcoming barriers to innovation in large organisations. Mike can be contacted at **www.mikekennard.com**.

Bibliography

- **Abernathy, W.J. and Clark, K.B.** (1985). Innovation: Mapping the Winds of Creative Destruction, *Research Policy*, 14(1), pp. 3–22.

- **Acs, Z. and Mueller, P.** (2008). Employment Effects of Business Dynamics: Mice, Gazelles and Elephants, *Small Business Economics,* 30(1), pp. 85–100.

- **Aggarwal, R.** (2010). Business Strategies for Multinational Intellectual Property Protection, *Thunderbird International Business Review*, 52(6), pp. 541–551.

- **Aldrich, H. and Herker, D.** (1977). Boundary Spanning Roles and Organisational Structure, *Academy of Management Review*, 2(2), pp. 217–230.

- **Ananad, B. and Galetovic, A.** (2004). How Market Smarts Can Protect Property Rights, *Harvard Business Review*, December, pp. 73–79.

- **Anderson, P. and Tushman, M.** (1990). Technological Discontinuities and Dominant Designs: A Cyclical Model of Technological Change, *Administrative Science Quarterly*, 35(4), pp. 604–633.

- **Anderson, C.** (2006). *The Long Tail: Why the Future of Business is Selling Less of More,* New York: Hyperion.

- **Anthony, S. and Christensen, C.** (2012). The Empires Strike Back: How Xerox and Other Large Corporations are Harnessing the Force of Disruptive Innovation, *Technology Review*, 115(1), pp. 66–68.

- **Arundel, A.** (2001). The Relative Effectiveness of Patents and Secrecy for Appropriation, *Research Policy*, 30(4), pp. 611–24.

BIBLIOGRAPHY

- **Baghai, M., Coley, S. and White, D.** (2000). *The Alchemy of Growth*, London: Texere.

- **Bainbridge, D.** (2012). *Intellectual Property*, 9th ed. London: Pearson.

- **Baptista, R. and Swann, P.** (1998). Do Firms in Clusters Innovate More?, *Research Policy*, 27(5), pp. 525–540.

- **Becker, R.H. and Speltz, L.M.** (1983). Putting the S-Curve Concept to Work, *Research Management*, 27(5), pp. 31-33.

- **Bell, G.** (2005). Clusters, Networks, and Firm Innovativeness, *Strategic Management Journal*, 26(3), pp. 287–295.

- **Birch, D.** (1981). Who Creates Jobs?, *The Public Interest*, 65, pp. 3–14.

- **Birch, D. L.** (1989). Change, Innovation, and Job Generation, *Journal of Labor Research*, 10(1), pp. 33–38.

- **Birkinshaw, J. and Gibson, C.** (2004). Building Ambidexterity into an Organization, *MIT Sloan Management Review*, 45(4), pp. 47–55.

- **Birkinshaw, J. and Mol, M.** (2006). How Management Innovation Happens, *MIT Sloan Management Review*, 47(4), pp. 81–88.

- **Birkinshaw, J., Hamel, G. and Mol, M.** (2008). Management Innovation, *Academy of Management Review*, 33(4), pp. 825–845.

- **Bjork, J., Boccardelli, P. and Magnusson, M.** (2010). Ideation Capabilities for Continuous Innovation, *Creativity and Innovation Management*, 19(4), pp. 385–396.

BIBLIOGRAPHY

- **Blackler, F.** (1995). Knowledge, Knowledge Work and Organizations: An Overview and Interpretation, *Organization Studies*, 16(60), pp. 1021–1046.

- **Bogers, M., A. Afuah, and B. Bastian.** (2010). Users as innovators: A review, critique and future research directions. *Journal of Management*, 36 (4), pp. 857–875.

- **Boulding, W. and Christen, M.** (2008). Disentangling Pioneering Cost Advantages and Disadvantages, *Marketing Science*, 27(4), pp. 699–716.

- **Bower J.L. and Christensen, C.** (1995). Disruptive Technologies: Catching the Wave, *Harvard Business Review*, 73(1), pp. 43–53.

- **Brand, A.** (1998). Knowledge Management and Innovation at 3M, *Journal of Knowledge Management*, 2(1), pp. 17–22.

- **Brynjolfsson, E., Hu, Y.J. and Smith, M.** (2006). From Niches to Riches: Anatomy of the Long Tail, *MIT Sloan Management Review*, 47(4), pp. 67–71.

- **Brynjolfsson, E., Hu, Y.J. and Simester, D.** (2011). Goodbye Pareto Principle, Hello Long Tail: The Effect of Search Costs on the Concentration of Product Sales, *Management Science*, 57(8), pp. 1373–1386.

- **Buisson, B. and Silberzahn, P.** (2010). Blue Ocean or Fast-Second Innovation? A Four-Breakthrough Model to Explain Successful Market Domination, *International Journal of Innovation Management*, 14(3), pp. 359–378.

- **Burgelman, R.A. and Välikangas, L.** (2005). Managing Internal Corporate Venturing Cycles, *MIT Sloan Management Review*, 46(4), pp. 26–34.

BIBLIOGRAPHY

- **Catmull, E.** (2008). How Pixar Fosters Collective Creativity, *Harvard Business Review*, 86(9), pp. 65–72.
- **Chesbrough, H.** (2000). Designing Corporate Ventures in the Shadow of Private Venture Capital, *California Management Review*, 42(3), pp. 31–49.
- **Chesbrough, H.** (2002). Making Sense of Corporate Venture Capital, *Harvard Business Review*, 80(3), pp. 90–99.
- **Chesbrough, H.** (2002). *Open Innovation; the new Imperative for Creating and Profiting from Technology*, Boston MA: Harvard Business School Press.
- **Chesbrough, H.** (2002). Graceful Exits and Missed Opportunities: Xerox's Management of its Technology Spin-Off Organisations, *Business History Review*, 76(4), pp. 803–837.
- **Chesbrough, H.** (2003). The Era of Open Innovation, *MIT Sloan Management Review*, 44(3), pp. 35–41.
- **Chesbrough, H.** (2007). Why companies should have open business models. *MIT Sloan Management Review*, 48(2), pp. 1–22.
- **Christensen, C.M.** (1992). Exploring the Limits of the Technology S-Curve. Part I: Component Technologies, *Production and Operations Management*, 1(4), pp. 334–357.
- **Christensen, C.M.** (1992). Exploring the Limits of the Technology S-Curve. Part II: Architectural Technologies, *Production and Operations Management*, 1(4), pp. 358–366.
- **Christensen, C.** (1997). *The Innovator's Dilemma: When New Technologies Cause Great Companies to Fail*, Boston, MA: Harvard Business School Press.

BIBLIOGRAPHY

- **Christensen, C. and Overdorf, M.** (2000). Meeting the Challenge of Disruptive Change, *Harvard Business Review*, 78(2), pp. 67–76.

- **Christensen, C., Johnson, M. and Rigby, D.** (2002). Foundations for Growth: How to Identify and Build Disruptive New Businesses, *MIT Sloan Management Review*, 43(3), pp. 22–31.

- **Christensen, C. and Raynor, M.** (2003). *The Innovator's Solution: Creating and Sustaining Successful Growth*, Boston, MA: Harvard Business School Press.

- **Clagett, R.P.** (1967). *Receptivity to Innovation – Overcoming N.I.H.*, Masters Thesis, Boston MA: MIT.

- **Cohen, W. and Levinthal, D.** (1990). Absorptive Capacity: A New Perspective on Learning and Innovation, *Administrative Science Quarterly*, 35, pp. 128–32.

- **Covin, J.G. and Miles, M.P.** (2007). Strategic Use of Corporate Venturing, *Entrepreneurship Theory and Practice*, 31(2), pp. 183–207.

- **Danneels, E.** (2004). Disruptive Technology Reconsidered: A Critique and Research Agenda, *Journal of Product Innovation Management*, 21(4), pp. 246–258.

- **David, P.** (1985). Clio and the Economics of QWERTY, *Economic History*, 75, pp. 332–357.

- **Drucker, P.** (1985). The Discipline of Innovation, *Harvard Business Review*, 63(3), pp. 67–72.

- **Drucker, P.** (1985). *Innovation and Entrepreneurship*, New York: Harper and Row.

BIBLIOGRAPHY

- **Duncan, R.** (1976). The Ambidextrous Organization: Designing Dual Structures for Innovation, In Killman, R.H., Pondy, L.R. and Sleven, D. (eds), *The Management of Organization*, 1, pp. 167–188. New York: North Holland.

- **Dyer, H. Gregersen, H. and Christensen, C.** (2009). The Innovator's DNA, *Harvard Business Review*, 90(4), pp. 92–102.

- **Etzkowitz, H. and Leydesdorff, L.** (1997). *Universities and the Global Knowledge Economy: A Triple Helix of University-Industry-Government Relations*, London: Cassell Academic.

- **Etzkowitz, H. and Leydesdorff, L.** (2000). The Dynamics of Innovation: From National Systems and 'Mode 2' to a Triple Helix of University-Industry-Government Relations, *Research Policy*, 29(2), pp. 109–123.

- **Etzkowitz, H.** (2011). Triple Helix Circulation: The Heart of Innovation and Development, *International Journal of Technology Management and Sustainable Development*, 7(2), pp. 101–115.

- **Fleming, L.** (2007). Breakthroughs and the Long Tail of Innovation, *MIT Sloan Management Review*, 49(1), pp. 69–74.

- **Foster, R.** (1986). *Innovation: The Attackers Advantage*, New York: Summit Books.

- **Freeman, J. and Engel, J.** (2007). Models of Innovation: Start-Ups and Mature Corporations, *California Management Review*, 50(1), pp. 94–119.

- **Gabaix, X.** (1999). Zipf's Law for Cities: An Explanation, *Quarterly Journal of Economics*, 114(3), pp. 739–767.

BIBLIOGRAPHY

- **Gallagher, S.** (2007). The Complementary Role of Dominant Designs and Industry Standards, *IEEE Transactions on Engineering Management*, 54(2), pp. 371–379.

- **Genus, A. and Coles, A.** (2006). Firm Strategies for Risk Management in Innovation, *International Journal of Innovation Management*, 10(2), pp. 113–126.

- **Geroski, P.** (2000). Models of Technology Diffusion, *Research Policy*, 29(4/5), pp. 603–625.

- **Gibbert, M. and Välikangas, L.** (2004). Boundaries and Innovation: Special Issue Introduction, *Long Range Planning*, 37(6), pp. 495–504.

- **Gladwell, M.** (2011). Creation Myth: Xerox PARC, Apple, and the Truth about Innovation, *The New Yorker*, 87(13), pp. 44–53.

- **Grant, R.** (1991). Porter's Competitive Advantage of Nations: An Assessment, *Strategic Management Journal*, 12(1), pp. 535–548.

- **Grant, R.M.** (1996). Towards a Knowledge Based Theory of the Firm, *Strategic Management Journal*, Winter Special Issue, pp. 109–122.

- **Hamel, G.** (1999). Bringing Silicon Valley Inside, *Harvard Business Review*, 77(5), pp. 70–84.

- **Hamel, G.** (2006). The Why, What, and How of Management Innovation, *Harvard Business Review*, 84(2), pp. 72–84.

- **Hansen, M., Nohria, N. and Tierney, T.** (1999). What's Your Strategy for Managing Knowledge? *Harvard Business Review*, 77(2), pp. 106–116.

BIBLIOGRAPHY

- **Hitzik, M.** (2000). *Dealers of Lightning: Xerox PARC and the Dawn of the Computer Age*, New York: Harper Business.

- **Huston, L. and Sakkab, N.** (2006). Connect and Develop: Inside P&Gs New Model for Innovation, *Harvard Business Review*, 84(3), pp. 58–66.

- **Intellectual Property Office** (2014). *Patents: Essential Reading*, Cardiff: Intellectual Property Office.

- **Isaacson, W.** (2011). *Steve Jobs: The Exclusive Biography*, New York: Simon & Schuster.

- **Isaacson, W.** (2012). The Real Leadership Lessons of Steve Jobs, *Harvard Business Review*, April, pp. 93–102.

- **Katz, R. and Allen, T.** (1982). Investigating the Not Invented Here (NIH) Syndrome: A Look at the Performance, Tenure, and Communication Patterns of 50 R&D Project Groups, *R&D Management*, 12(1), pp. 7–19.

- **Kahneman, D., Lovallo, D. and Sibony, O.** (2011). Before You Make That Big Decision…, *Harvard Business Review*, June, pp. 50–60.

- **Kerin R., Varadarajan, R. and Peterson, R.** (1992). First Mover Advantage: A Synthesis, Conceptual Framework, and Research Propositions, *Journal of Marketing*, 56(4), pp. 33–52.

- **Kim, W. and Mauborgne, R.** (2004). Blue Ocean Strategy, *Harvard Business Review*, 82(10), pp. 76–84.

- **Kim, W. and Mauborgne, R.** (2005). Blue Ocean Strategy: From Theory to Practice, *California Management Review*, 47(3), pp. 105–121.

BIBLIOGRAPHY

- **Kim, W. and Mauborgne, R.** (2005). Value Innovation: A Leap into the Blue Ocean, *Journal of Business Strategy*, 26(4), pp. 22–28.

- **Kim, W. and Mauborgne, R.** (2005). *Blue Ocean Strategy: How to Create Uncontested Market Space and Make the Competition Irrelevant*. Boston MA: Harvard Business School Press.

- **Kondratiev, N.** (1935). The Long Waves in Economic Life, *Review of Economic Statistics*, 17, pp. 6–105.

- **Korotayev, A., Zinkina, J. and Bogevolnov, J.** (2011). Kondratieff Waves in Global Invention Activity, *Technological Forecasting and Social Change*, 78(7), pp. 1280–1284.

- **Laden, K.** (1996). Not Invented There, or, the Other Persons Dessert Always Looks Better!, *Research Technology Management*, 39, pp. 10–12.

- **Leifer, R., McDermott C., O'Connor, G., Peters, L., Rice, M., and Veryzer, R.** (2000). *Radical Innovation: How Mature Companies Can Outsmart Upstarts*, Boston MA: Harvard Business School Press.

- **Leydesdorff, L., Etzkowitz, H.** (1996). Emergence of a Triple Helix of University–Industry–Government Relations, *Science and Public Policy*, 23, pp. 279–286.

- **Leydesdorff, L., Etzkowitz, H.** (1998). The Triple Helix as a Model for Innovation Studies, *Science and Public Policy* 25(3), pp. 195–203.

- **Leydesdorff, L.** (2000). The Triple Helix: An Evolutionary Model of Innovations, *Research Policy*, 29(2), pp. 243–256.

- **Lichtenthaler, U. and Ernst, H.** (2006). Attitudes to Externally Organising Knowledge Management Tasks: A Review, Reconsideration and Extension of the NIH Syndrome, *R&D Management*, 36(4), pp. 367–386.

- **Lichtenthaler, U.** (2011). Open Innovation: Past Research, Current Debates, and Future Directions, *Academy of Management Perspectives*, 25(1), pp. 75–93.

- **Lieberman, M. and Montgomery, D.** (1988). First Mover Advantages, *Strategic Management Journal*, 9, pp. 41–58.

- **Lieberman, M. and Montgomery, D.** (1998). First Mover (Dis) Advantages: Retrospective and Link with the Resource Based View, *Strategic Management Journal*, 19(12), pp. 1111–1125.

- **Liebowitz, S. and Margolis, S.** (1990). The Fable of the Keys, *Journal of Law and Economics*, 33(1), pp. 1–26.

- **Loutfy, R. and Belkhir, L.** (2001). Managing Innovation at Xerox, *Research Technology Management*, 44(4), pp. 15–25.

- **Mahajan, V. and Muller, E.** (1998). When is it Worthwhile Targeting the Majority Instead of the Innovators in a New Product Launch? *Journal of Marketing Research*, 35, pp. 488–495.

- **March, J.G.** (1991). Exploration and Exploitation in Organizational Learning, *Organization Science*, 2, pp. 71–87.

- **Markides, C** (2006). Disruptive Innovation: In Need of Better Theory, *Journal of Product Innovation Management*, 23(1), pp. 19–25.

- **Martin, R. and Sunley, P.** (2003). Deconstructing Clusters: Chaotic Concept or Policy Panacea?, *Journal of Economic Geography*, 3, pp. 5–35.

- **Martins, E. and Terblanche, F.** (2003). Building Organisational Culture that Stimulates Creativity and Innovation, *European Journal of Innovation Management*, 6(1), pp. 64–74.

BIBLIOGRAPHY

- **McDermott, C. and O'Connor G.** (2002). Managing Radical Innovation: An Overview of Emergent Strategy Issues, *Journal of Product Innovation Management*, 19(1), pp. 424–438.

- **McGrath, R., Keil, T. and Tukiainen, T.** (2006). Extracting Value from Corporate Venturing, *MIT Sloan Management Review*, 48(1), pp. 50–56.

- **McLaughlin, P., Bessant, J., and Smart, P.** (2008). Developing an Organisational Culture to Facilitate Radical Innovation, *International Journal of Technology Management*, 44(3/4), pp. 298–322.

- **Menon, T. and Pfeffer, J.** (2003). Valuing Internal vs. External Knowledge: Explaining the Preference for Outsiders, *Management Science*, 49, pp. 497–513.

- **Moore, G.** (1991). *Crossing the Chasm: Marketing and Selling High-Tech Products to Mainstream Customers*, New York: Harper Business.

- **Moore, G.** (2004). Darwin and the Demon: Innovating Within Established Enterprises, *Harvard Business Review*, July, pp. 87–92.

- **Moore, G.** (2006). *Dealing with Darwin: How Great Companies Innovate at Every Phase of Their Evolution*, Chichester: Wiley.

- **Moore, G.** (2007). To Succeed in the Long Term, Focus on the Middle Term, *Harvard Business Review*, 85(7/8), pp. 84–90.

- ***Nagji, B. and Tuff, G.*** (2012). Managing Your Innovation Portfolio, *Harvard Business Review*, 90(5), pp. 66–74.

- **Napp, J.J. and Minshall, T.** (2011). Corporate Venture Capital Investments for Enhancing Innovation: Challenges and Solutions, *Research Technology Management*, March-April, pp. 27–36.

- **O'Reilly III, C.H. and Tushman, M.L.** (2004). The Ambidextrous Organisation, *Harvard Business Review,* 82(4), pp. 74–81.

- **Pisano, G. and Teece, D.** (2007). How to Capture Value from Innovation: Shaping Intellectual Property and Industry Architecture, *California Management Review*, 50(1), pp. 278–296.

- **Plessis, M.** (2007). The Role of Knowledge Management in Innovation, *Journal of Knowledge Management*, 55(6), pp. 49–57.

- **Porter, M.E.** (1998). Clusters and the New Economies of Competition, *Harvard Business Review*, 76(6), pp. 77–90.

- **Porter, M.E.** (1990). *The Competitive Advantage of Nations*, New York: Free Press.

- **Raisch, S. and Birkinshaw, J.** (2008). Organisational Ambidexterity: Antecedents, Outcomes, and Moderators, *Journal of Management*, 34(3), pp. 375–409.

- **Raisch, S., Birkinshaw, J., Probst, G. and Tushman, M.L.** (2009). Organisational Ambidexterity: Balancing Exploitation and Exploration for Sustained Performance, *Organization Science*, 20(4), pp. 685–695.

- **Ram, S. and Jung, H.** (1994). Innovativeness in Product Usage: A Comparison of Early Adopters and Early Majority, *Psychology and Marketing*, 11(1), pp. 57–67.

- **Reitzig, M.** (2004). Strategic Management of Intellectual Property, *MIT Sloan Management Review*, 45(3), pp. 35–40.

- **Reitzig, M., Henkel, J. and Heath, C.** (2007). On Sharks, Trolls, and Their Patent Prey – Unrealistic Damage Awards and Firms' Strategies of 'Being Infringed', *Research Policy*, 36(1), pp. 134–154.

BIBLIOGRAPHY

- **Rivette, K. and Kline, D.** (2000). *Rembrandts in the Attic: Unlocking the Hidden Value of Patents*, Boston MA: Harvard Business School Press.

- **Rogers, E.M.** (1958). Categorizing the Adopters of Agricultural Practices, *Rural Sociology*, 23(1), pp. 345–354.

- **Rogers, E.M.** (2003). *Diffusion of Innovations*, 5th ed., New York: Free Press.

- **Rosenzweig, P.** (2007). *The Halo Effect and Eight Other Business Delusions that Deceive Managers*, New York: Free Press.

- **Rothwell, R. and Gardiner, P.** (1985). Invention, Innovation, Re-Invention and the Role of the User, *Technovation*, 3, pp. 167–186.

- **Santos, F. and Eisenhardt, K.** (2005). Organizational Boundaries and Theories of Organization. Organization Science, 16 (5): 491–508.

- **Schumpeter, J.A.** (1934). *The Theory of Economic Development: An Inquiry into Profits, Capital, Credit, Interest, and the Business Cycle*, New Brunswick: Transaction Books.

- **Schumpeter, J.A.** (1939). *Business Cycles: A Theoretical, Historical, and Statistical Analysis of the Capitalist Process*, New York: McGraw-Hill.

- **Schumpeter, J.A.** (1942). *Capitalism, Socialism, and Democracy*, New York: Harper.

- **Schilling, M.A. and Esmundo, M.** (2009). Technology S-Curves in Renewable Energy Alternatives: Analysis and Implications for Industry and Government, *Energy Policy*, 37, pp. 1767–1781.

- **Schmidt, G. and Druel, C.** (2008). When is Disruptive Innovation Disruptive? *The Journal of Product Innovation Management*, 25(4), pp. 347–369.

- **Shankar, V., Carpenter, G.S. and Krishnamurthi, L.** (1988). Late Mover Advantage: How Innovative Late Entrants Outsell Pioneers, *Journal of Marketing Research*, 35, pp. 54–70.

- **Shapiro, C. and Varian, H.R.** (1999). The Art of Standard Wars, *California Management Review*, 41(2), pp. 8–32.

- **Slater, S.F., Mohr, J.J. and Sengupta, S.** (2014). Radical Product Innovation Capability: Literature Review, Synthesis, and Illustrative Research Propositions, *Journal of Product Innovation Management*, 31(3), pp. 552–566.

- **Smihula, D.** (2010). Waves of Technological Innovations and the end of the Industrial Revolution, *Journal of Economics and International Finance*, 2(4), pp. 58–67.

- **Smith, D.K, and Alexander, R.C.** (1988). *Fumbling the future: How Xerox Invented, and then Ignored, the First Personal Computer*, New York: Morrow.

- **Spencer, A., Kirchhoff, B. and White, C.** (2008). Entrepreneurship, Innovation, and Wealth Distribution: The Essence of Creative Destruction, *International Small Business Journal*, 26(1), pp. 9–26.

- **Suarez, F.F.** (1999). Battles for Technological Dominance: An Integrative Framework, *Research Policy*, 33, pp. 271–286.

- **Suarez, F. and Lanzolla, G.** (2005). The Half Truth of First Mover Advantage, *Harvard Business Review*, 83(4), pp. 121–127.

BIBLIOGRAPHY

- **Trott, P. and Hartmann, D.** (2009). Why 'Open Innovation' is Old Wine in New Bottles, *International Journal of Innovation Management*, 13(4), pp. 715–736.
- **Tushman, M.** (1977). Special Boundary Roles in the Innovation Process, *Administrative Science Quarterly*, 22(4), pp. 587–605.
- **Tushman, M. and Scanlan, T.** (1981). Characteristics and External Orientations of Boundary Spanning Individuals, *Academy of Management Journal*, 24(1), pp. 83–98.
- **Urban, G. and von Hippel, E.** (1988). Lead User Analyses for the Development of New Industrial Products, *Management Science*, 34(5), pp. 569–582.
- **Utterback, J.M. and Abernathy, W.J.** (1975). A Dynamic Model of Process and Product Innovation, *Omega*, 3, pp. 639–656.
- **Utterback, J.M.** (1994). *Mastering the Dynamics of Innovation: How Companies Can Seize Opportunities in the Face of Technological Change*, Boston MA: Harvard Business School Press.
- **Utterback, J.M.** (1995). Dominant Designs and the Survival of Firms, *Strategic Management Journal*, 16(6), pp. 415–430.
- **Vaitheeswaren, V. and Carson, I.** (2007). Special Report on Innovation: The Fading Lustre of Clusters, *The Economist*, October 13th-19th, pp. 20-23.
- **von Hippel, E.** (1978). Users as Innovators, *Technology Review*, 80(3), pp. 30-34.
- **von Hippel, E.** (1986). Lead Users: A Source of Novel Product Concepts, *Management Science*, 32(7), pp. 791–805.

BIBLIOGRAPHY

- **von Hippel, E.** (1988). *The Sources of Innovation*, New York: Oxford University Press.

- **von Hippel, E.** (2005). *Democratizing Innovation*, Cambridge MA: MIT Press.

- **Woodman, R.W., Sawyer, J.E. and Griffin, R.W.** (1993). Toward a Theory of Organizational Creativity. *Academy of Management Review*, 18 (2), pp. 293–321.

- **Zack, M.H.** (1999). Developing a Knowledge Strategy, *California Management Journal*, 5, pp. 125–145.

- **Zahra, M. and George, G.** (2002). Absorptive Capacity: A Review, Reconceptualization, and Extension, *Academy of Management Review*, 27, pp. 185–203.

- **Zipf, G.** (1949). *Human Behaviour and the Principle of Least Effort*, Cambridge MA: Addison Wesley.